GOD'S ANGELS IN DISGUISE

Blessed Is He Who Considers The Poor,
The Lord will deliver him in time of trouble.

VOLUME 2

MARIE E. WILLIAMSON

Order this book online at www.trafford.com
or email orders@trafford.com

Most Trafford titles are also available at major online book retailers.

 www.trafford.com

North America & international
toll-free: 844 688 6899 (USA & Canada)
fax: 812 355 4082

Our mission is to efficiently provide the world's finest, most comprehensive book publishing service, enabling every author to experience success. To find out how to publish your book, your way, and have it available worldwide, visit us online at www.trafford.com

Because of the dynamic nature of the Internet, any web addresses or links contained in this book may have changed since publication and may no longer be valid. The views expressed in this work are solely those of the author and do not necessarily reflect the views of the publisher, and the publisher hereby disclaims any responsibility for them.

Any people depicted in stock imagery provided by Getty Images are models, and such images are being used for illustrative purposes only.
Certain stock imagery © Getty Images.

ISBN: 978-1-6987-0695-5 (sc)

ISBN: 978-1-6987-0694-8 (e)

Print information available on the last page.

Trafford rev. 05/18/2021

CONTENTS

TRIBUTE & HONOR TO GOD

Lord, You Are the Bishop of my soul. 1 Peter 2:25 states, "For ye were as sheep going astray; but are now returned unto the Shepherd and Bishop of your souls," to my King Jesus who is always so GENEROUS, towards me in His giving not sparingly, but gives to me in abundance, so I can bless others. Jesus your FAITHFULNESS, towards me as captivate my attention and brought me to a place of not understanding You at all, when I thought that I was just beginning to learn who You are, and how you work in my life. Father your PATIENCE for me; out way anything I have ever experience in life. When I mess up, You simply come back and gently correct me, and lead me back on the right path. At times, I give up on You, however; you kept your patience, and explain how much You love me. Papa Jesus, You are WORTHY, of all the *praises, worship* that You fill my heart with. You are WORTHY for all the persecution; I have gone through and will experience. Just, because You love me so much. For Christ, I live and for Christ I will die. God how EXCELLENT, You are in my life. My daily living is a challenge, but with Your presence, it is always well. Lord, just because You are a great LISTENER, I am a better person today. Few people take the time to listen to each other problems, or try to find a way to help them, but You Lord, You do it so well. Lord, You listen. When I am not well, when I have a story to tell. When I have a case to present. When burdens overwhelm me. What is best is when You listen to my heart's silent cries. You, listen when I worship, sing, and pray. Lord, you listen so well, as I often told You, LORD YOU ARE THE BEST LISTENER IN THE WORLD. Acts 16:25 reads, "And at midnight Paul and Silas prayed, and sang praises unto God: and the prisoners heard them." "How you do it so well." "I can't tell", but this one thing I know I appreciate it well.

BREAK-OUT! BREAK-THROUGH!

THANK YOU, LORD, FOR THE WORDS YOU GAVE ME IN 2018 TO SUSTAIN ME AND MY FAMILY. THANK YOU FOR HEALING ME FROM FRIBRIODS.

2021 THE BEST IS YET TO COME! LIVE IN THE MOMENT! IT IS WELL!

ACKNOWLEDGMENTS

With special acknowledgments to Aunt Linda, who has been a second Mom. One who exemplify the love of God and is extremely compassionate when helping God's people. In fact, she enjoys assisting individuals who are having a difficult time in life and need a home.

Next my respected mother Watson, God bless you so much for all your love and encouragement during the many storms I face in 2014- 2018. Second, for praying me through, God always has a person caught in the thicket. Third, baby Chloe, thank God for your miraculous birth in 2013, which taught us that God could bring a 1.6-pound baby into this world. And sustain her to live and celebrated her 4th birthday September 29/2017.

Above all, my wonderful mom (Rosetta Walker) thank you for bringing me into this world, your love, prayers, and support has kept me. Next, Franklin Campbell my precious cousin one who inspires me to believe in God, and myself that I can achieve and aspire to great things in this world. Second, I cannot forget Monica Jones, thank you for backing me to complete my second work which push me into my destiny.

Third, much thanks to Sister Karen who was passionate about my first book. Which brought me into greater understanding of what writing about my adventures with Christ as meant to the body of Christ. Thanks to those, who read my book and commented, it brought me to another level of consciousness of what God is doing through me with His special gift. Your perspectives have blessed my life beyond your wildest imaginations. (Dreams) Last but least, to Bishop and Lady Smith who has been an inspiration in my Christian journey with God. Their life experiences they shared with me in the ministry and in counseling as effected my life so much. It teaches me to reach for whatever God as for me, which is considerably greater than my imagination. From their humble beginning, to how God as established them which exemplify their love and faithfulness toward Almighty God. Their spiritual nurturing, advice, and great leadership style will leave a lasting impact on the rest of my life no matter where life takes me. Their kindness is beyond this world. I often prayed and asked God not to let others take advantage of their kindness.

Finally, Pastor Franklin Williamson my cousin I thank God for you .

This book was process and established through the divine help and inspiration of the Holy Spirit.

POEM
WHAT IS A GIFT?
8/4/2018 9:03 p.m.

A gift is bought.
A gift is given.
A gift comes from heaven.
A gift is dwelling within.
Just waiting to be discovered.
Where is your gift hidden?
Do you know?
Do you care?
Is your gift from heaven?
Is it just there just waiting to be discovered?

POEM
MY LOVE IS MORE THAN YOUR LOVE LORD

My love is more than your Lord,
because I have to go through sickness and pain.
My love for you is more than your love for me,
because you did not feel the pain,
I am feeling now.
Have you felt this pain?
Have you carried fibroids in your womb?
My love for you is more than your love for me.
You were crucified yes! But the fibroid pain I am feeling,
my love is more than you love me.
Lord can you proof yourself to me.
My Love is more than your love lord. My life is a testimony.
My love for you is more than your love for me,
because I have born some pain that a woman should never have to bear.
I am not Adam and I am not eve but because they sin have to take that pain.
My love is more than your love.
My love is more than your love.
I am waiting for you to proof your love.
Did you say, you bore my sins and took my pain?
Well tell me tell me.
How can my love be more than your love for me?
I just have a quick, quick, quick, testimony.
How can my love be more than you love?
Jesus?
When you said you were wounded for my transgression?

bruise for my iniquity and the chastisement of my peace was upon you.
And by your stripes I am heal.
The spirit of the Lord is upon you and with his stripes I am
heal how can my love be more than your love.
Lord can you proof that to me so I can have a real testimony.
Kiss! I love you Lord

SONG
YOUR PLAN FOR MY LIFE! I AM A LIVE
8/9/2018 6:24pm

I pray each day I arise, that I may see your plan.
I pray each day I arise, that I may see your plan.
I pray each day I arise, that I may see your plan.
See your see your plan for my life.
I pray each day I live, that I may see your hand.
I pray each day I live, that I may see your gracious hand.
I pray each day I live, that I may see your blessed hand.
See your hand see your hand in my life.
I pray each day that I arise that I may hear your voice, hear your voice speaking crystal clear for my life.
I pray each day that I arise that I may hear your voice, hear your voice for my life.
Each day that I arise that I may hear your voice, hear your voice for my life.
Tomorrow is not promise but thank God today I am alive.
Tomorrow is not promise but thank God today I am alive.
My tomorrow is not promise but thank God today I am alive. I am alive.
I am alive.
I am alive.
I am free
I am free, Jesus lives in me
I am alive.
I am alive.
I am alive.
I am alive.

SONG
PRAISE THE LORD
3/28/17

I got a dream to tell the story.
I got a dream praise the Lord.
I got a dream that Jesus gave me.
I got a dream, for He is Holy.
I got a dream to tell the story.
I got a dream praise the Lord.

HE WILL DO IT AGAIN
8:45pm 7/13/17

He will do it again, hold me closer to his side.
I may not know which way to go.
He knows the way.
He will do it again, hold me closer to his side.
I may not know which way to go.
He knows the way.
He knows the way.
He knows the way.
God knows the way he will do it again.
I may not know which way to go, but he knows the way.
He knows the way.
I may not know which way to go but He knows the way.
He knows the way.

SONG
THE KING
5/7/17

What do you give to the King who as everything?
Diamonds and pearls, he does not need a thing.
Silver and gold, rubies, and pearls, He owns everything.
He owns, the wealth of this world in His hand.
You bring, worship to the King.
The King of kings.
Worship, worship worship to the King.
You bring, worship to the King.
The King of Kings.
He owns the wealth of his world in His hands.
My offering to the King is worship.
I bring worship to my King.
He don't need a thing.
Just worship, worship worship.
You bring worship, worship to the King.
Worship, worship, worship.

JESUS AND ME
5/7/17 1:53am

My tomorrow will be a glorious day.
My tomorrow will be a glorious day.
My tomorrow will be a glorious day.
I hope you wait and see,
For it will be for me.
For it will be for me.
For it will be for me.
My tomorrow will be a beautiful day
My tomorrow will be a beautiful day
My tomorrow will be a beautiful day
My tomorrow will be a beautiful day
I hope you wait and see,
For it will be for me.
For it will be for me.
For it will be for me.
I hope you wait and see,
For it will be for me.
For it will be for me.
For it will be for me.

My tomorrow will be an amazing day.
My tomorrow will be an amazing day.
My tomorrow will be an amazing day.

I hope you wait and see,
For it will be for me.
For it will be for me.
For it will be for me.

My tomorrow will be a wondrous day.
My tomorrow will be a wondrous day
My tomorrow will be a wondrous day

I hope you wait and see,
For it will be for me.
For it will be for me.
For it will be for me.
My tomorrow will be an excellent day.
My tomorrow will be an excellent day.
My tomorrow will be an excellent day.
I hope you wait and see,
For it will be for me.
For it will be for me.
For it will be for me.
My tomorrow will be just for me.
My tomorrow will be just for Jesus and me.
Jesus and I will heal the sick today,
Just you wait and see.
Jesus and I will raise the dead today,
Jesus and I will cleanse the leaper today,
Just you wait and see.
My tomorrow will be a wondrous day
Tomorrow will be a special day.
Tomorrow will be sun shinny day.
Just you wait and see.
Tomorrow will be a glorious day.
My tomorrow will be for Jesus and me.
Jesus and I will go along the narrow way.
Jesus and I will live in eternity today.
My tomorrow will be a victorious day.
My tomorrow will be a manifesting day.
Tomorrow will be Jesus and me.
My tomorrow will be an excellent day.
Jesus and I will laugh and play.
Jesus and I will love always.
Jesus and I will cry today.
Tomorrow will be just for me.
My tomorrow will be my destiny.

Jesus and I will laugh and play.
Jesus and I will go along the narrow way.
My tomorrow will be just for me.
Just you wait and see.

MY SHEKINAH-GLORY
2/7/17

Jesus, you are my Shekinah glory
That is who you are
I will praise you
I will praise you
I will praise you
I adore you
I adore you
Oh, how I love you
My Shekinah glory that is who you are
I will praise you
I will praise you
I will praise you
Jesus, you are my Shekinah glory that is who you are
I will worship you
I will worship you
I will worship you
I adore you
I adore you
My Shekinah glory I know who you are
I adore you
I adore you
My Shekinah glory that is who you are
My Shekinah glory that is who you are
My Shekinah glory that is who you are
My Shekinah glory Jesus I need you.

SONG
A GOOD STEWART
5/8/17 8:00am

My Father he will see me as a good Stewart.
My season is here.
My Father is here.
I am a good Stewart.
What does a good Stewart do with his or her
Time, money, love, anointing, calling, talent, prophecy,
inheritance, faith, word of God, giving, Holy Ghost,

WHY DID I WRITE THIS BOOK?

<u>Social justice</u>- unfair distribution of wealth, opportunities, and privileges within a society.
Bring awareness to the needy in my community and around the world
in efforts to help them get out of the condition they are living in.
Be a voice for them, an (advocate) act on some one's behalf represent,
disadvantage, and the best interest of someone). (Human rights)
What do you expect to gain from writing this book?
Change in how society views the needy.
Support from mayors of Newark, New Jersey
and all mayors in New Jersey.
Citizens needy themselves (organized)
7. Why am I doing this "? To the Lord he responded, "Is there not a cause?" (1 Samuel 17:29) "And
David said, what have I done? Is there not a cause? Is there anything too hard for God? God can
deliver one from poverty and, health issues? Just read (Jerimiah 32 :27) God responded to Jerimiah
the prophet after he prayed to God about the children of Israel has, they are going in to exile in
Babylon.

DEFINITIONS

<u>Homelessness</u>- There is more than one official definition of homelessness. Health centers funded by the U.S. Department of Health and Human Services (HHS) use the following:

A homeless individual is defined in section 330(h) (5) as an "individual who lacks housing (without regard to whether the individual is a member of a family), including and individual whose primary resident during the night is supervise in a public or private facility (e.g., shelters) that provides temporary living accommodations, and an individual who is in transitional housing." A homeless person is an individual without permanent housing who may be homeless: stay in a shelter, mission, single room occupancy facilities, abandoned building or vehicle; or in any other unstable or non- permanent situation. [Section330 Public Health Services Act (42 U.S.C., 254b)].

<u>PROCLIVITY</u> – A Tendency to Choose or Do Something Regularly: An Inclination or Predisposition Toward a Thing Worship God, Hard Work.

<u>Revivalist</u>- An evangelist who preaches to revive others.

<u>*Ingenuity*</u> - skill or cleverness in devising or combining: inventiveness: cleverness or aptness

WHO ARE ANGELS?

Angels are functional spiritual beings who assist us in our daily living, such as protection and influence. When Jesus Christ returns for His church, He will come back with His most powerful angels. (2 Thessalonians 1 :7- 10) "And to you who are troubled rest with us, when the Lord Jesus shall be revealed from heaven with his mighty angels." "When he shall come to be glorified in his saints, and to be admired in all them that believe (because our testimony among you were believe) in that day."

Luke 24 1-6 says, "Now upon the first day of the week, very early in the morning, they came unto the sepulcher, bringing the spices which they had prepared, and certain others came with them. And they found the stone rolled away from the sepulcher. And they entered in and found not the body of the Lord Jesus. And it came to pass, as they were much perplexed thereabout, behold two men stood by them in shining garments. And as they were afraid, and bowed down their faces to the earth, they said unto them, why seek ye the living among the dead? He is not here but is risen remember how he spake unto you when he was yet in Galilee."

This passage tells us that angels are powerful being and control- nature because God works through them to bring forth His glorious majestic works. Psalm 18 :7- 12, describes God and the angels has such "Then the earth shook and trembled; the foundation of the hill also quaked and were shaken, because He was angry. Smoke went up from His nostrils, and devouring fire from His mouth; coals were kindled by it. He bowed the heavens also and came down with darkness under his feet. And He did rode upon a cherub, and flew, He flew upon the wings of the wind, He made darkness His secret place, His canopy around Him was dark waters. And thick clouds of the skies. From the brightness before Him, His thick clouds passed with hailstones and coals of fire."

Revelation 7 : 1 says, "And after theses I saw four angels standing on the four corners of the earth, holding the four winds of the earth, that the wind should not blow on the earth, nor on the sea, nor on any tree."

Revelation 8: 12 says, "And the fourth angels sounded, and the third part of the sun was smitten, and the third part of the moon, and the third part of the starts; so as the third part of them was darkened, and the day shone not for a third part of it, and the night likewise."

God ride upon the cherubs to produces lightening thunder activities, and hailstones. God creates and moves through angels' activities.

LOOK WHAT THE LORD HAS DONE!

It is a pleasure to be engaged in street ministry!

The compassionate Ministry and THE needs of others.

**EDITOR
GRAPHIC DESIGNER
AND PHOTOGRAPHER**

Marie E. Williamson

Favorite Quotes by African American Activists and Bible Facts

Harriet Tubman Activist

"Every great dream begins with a dreamer. Always remember, you have within you the strength, the patience, and the passion to reach for the stars to change the world."

"I freed thousands of slaves, and could have freed thousands more, if they had known they were slaves."

"If you hear the dogs, keep going. If you see the torches in the woods, keep going. If there's shouting after you, keep going. Do not ever stop. Keep going. If you want a taste of freedom, keep going."

"Twant me, 'twas the Lord. I always told him, 'I trust to you. I do not know where to go or what to do, but I expect you to lead me,' and He always did."

"I had reasoned this out in my mind; there was one of two things I had a right to, liberty or death; if I could not have one, I would have the other; for no man should take me alive."

Tabitha (Dorcas),

A Woman of Energy, Grace, Beauty, and Quick Movements. Tabitha (Dorcas), Full of Good Works and Alms Did Continually. Help Poor and Needy in Her Community. And Became Sick Died and Was Rose from The Dead by Peter. Who Took Her Hand and Said a Rise! (Acts) (9:36-42

Phyllis Wheatley

In every human breast, God has implanted a Principle, which we call Love of Freedom; it is impatient of Oppression, and pants for Deliverance.
Read more at: http://www.azquotes.com/author/25162-Phillis_Wheatley

<u>Fredrick Douglas</u>

It is easier to build strong children than to repair broken men.
Without a struggle, there can be no progress.
Read more at: <u>http://www.azquotes.com/quote/81114</u>

<u>Sojourner Truth</u> Activist

Life is a hard battle anyway. If we laugh and sing a little as we fight the good fight of freedom, it makes it all go easier. I will not allow my life's light to be determined by the darkness around me.
Read more at: <u>http://www.azquotes.com/author/14828-Sojourner_Truth</u>

And ain't I a woman? Look at me! Look at my arm! I have ploughed and planted, and gathered into barns, and no man could head me! And ain't I a woman? I could work as much and eat as much as a man - when I could get it - and bear the lash as well! And ain't I a woman? I have borne thirteen children, and seen most all sold off to slavery, and when I cried out with my mother's grief, none but Jesus heard me! And ain't I a woman?
Read more at: <u>http://www.azquotes.com/author/14828-Sojourner_Truth</u>

<u>When I left the house of bondage, I left everything behind. I was not going to keep nothing of Egypt on me, an' so I went to the Lord an' asked him to give me a new name. And he gave me Sojourner because I was to travel up and down the land showing the people their sins and bein' a sign unto them. I told the Lord I wanted two names cause everybody else had two, and the Lord gave me Truth, because I was to declare the truth to the people.</u>

<u>Sojourner Truth</u>Read more at: <u>http://www.azquotes.com/author/14828-Sojourner_Truth</u>

Favorite Quotes from Other Influential

Leaders
Mother Theresa
"I know God won't give me anything I can't handle.
I just wish he didn't trust me so much."

"I have decided to stick to love
hate is too great a burden to bear"
"Forgiveness is not an occasional act.
It is a constant attitude"

"Live simply so others may simply live."
Live within your means and give the excess that God has blessed you with to help the less fortunate. You can put this quote into action by putting a budget and giving plan in place.

"Prayer is not asking. Prayer is putting oneself in the hands of God, at His disposition, and listening to His voice in the depth of our hearts."
Too often, we pray for how we want God to answer something rather than surrender to God and His will. Remember when praying today to do it in complete surrender.

"I can do things you cannot, you can do things I cannot; together we can do great things."
We are each part of the body of Christ and gifted in different areas. Act on the gifts that God has given you and start today.

"God doesn't require us to succeed, he only requires that you try."
Colossians 3:23 whatever *you do, work heartily, as for the Lord and not for men,*
Work hard today and do it for the glory of God!

For more quotes by Mother Teresa you can check out one of these articles:
http://www.whatchristianswanttoknow.com/mother-teresa-quotes-21-thoughtful-sayings/
http://www.goodreads.com/author/quotes/838305.Mother_Teresa

Benjamin Franklin
'Either write something worth reading or do something worth writing.'
'Three may keep a secret, if two of them are dead.

DEDICATION

This book is dedicated to the poor and needy who lives in our society and are rejected and despised due to their status. According to the Quick facts, a survey was done by the States Census Bureau of New Jersey, statistic shows that in 2010, blacks in Newark or African American alone were at 52.4% of homelessness population versus their white counterpart's population, which was at 26.3%. Besides the United States of America as 3.5 million homeless people, and the UK as 60,000. In brief, the homeless epidemic population is worldwide for instance in Jamaica West Indies, there are a total of 1,500 visible homeless people. Some of which are children 800 and adult men 650. However, there are foundations such as "Food for the Poor," that feeds the needy on the streets. The four parish which are affected most by homelessness in Jamaica are Saint James, Saint Ann, Saint Catherine, and Jamaica's capitol Kingston. Now that there is a "Pandemic cause by COVID-19 VIRUS" is creating a health and economic crisis in America worldwide on the most vulnerable population. The state of crisis before the COVID-19 was seventeen out of ever 10,000 people in the United States.

> "Blessed is he that considered the poor: the LORD will deliver him in the time of trouble (psalms 41-1).

Nonetheless, this book will also articulate, and demonstrates how the poor and needy in America were experiencing homelessness on average ever night from January 2019. **God's Angels in Disguise** and in deed a blessing. Furthermore, I could not have attained such knowledge had I not stepped out of my comfort zone and helped someone who was impoverished as God directed. With this in mind, without the influence and love of the Holy Ghost dwelling in my heart, I could not have written this book. In my daily walk with God, I always apply the scripture; "Trust in the Lord with all thine heart; and lean not unto thine own understanding. In all thy ways acknowledge Him and He shall direct thy paths (Proverbs 3:5- 6)." Likewise, I give all glory and honor to the Almighty God of heaven who had trained me and has given me a compassionate heart for the need of others. According to God's word, He instructs us to consider the poor, and he will reward us. Psalms 41 reads,

Blessed is he that considered the poor: the LORD will deliver him in the time of trouble. The LORD will preserve him, and keep him alive, and he shall be blessed upon the earth: and thou wilt not deliver him unto the will of his enemies. The LORD will strengthen him upon the bed of languishing: thou wilt make all his bed in his sickness (Psalms 41: 1-3).

Furthermore, it is no secret that the poor and needy are marginalized and denied involvement in mainstream economic, political, cultural, and social activities. They are scorned at times because they live below the poverty level. Many of those who have achieved social status such as education, and wealth, and are living the American dream, believe that the poor and needy are a nuisance. But, in fact little do they know that according to God's Holy Bible, the less fortunate are a blessing in society. Remember God said in His word, it is more blessed to give than to receive. As Paul, the apostle wrote to the Ephesian elders of the church, "I have shewed you all things, how that so laboring ye ought to support the weak, and remember the word of the Lord Jesus, how he said, it is more blessed to give than to receive" (Acts 20:35). Here the apostle Paul is exhorting the saints in Christ to give earnestly from their heart to the saints who are weak and in need. Paul does this by example because he too has an earnest passion for the brethren in Christ. His love enables him to apply his service whole heartedly without asking for monetary support. Moreover, by assisting the needy and encouraging someone in life, it may just lead one into their God-given destiny. Also, our Heavenly Father says in His words whatever we do to the least of these, we do it unto Him. to sum it up, if there is no one to give to in our society, how will we receive back from God and prove that His promises are true? In fact, they are the one's God uses to bring about our purpose in life. Notwithstanding, I have experience that His promises are true, and one to be appreciated and honor. Definitely, the poor are here for a purpose just like all of us, and our responsibility is to be our brother's keeper, and not judge them. As stated in Acts chapter 20, the bible says do unto others as we would want to be done to you. Likewise, our reward comes from God and not man.

According to Matthew 25

"When the Son of man shall come in his glory, and all the holy angels with him, then shall he sit upon the throne of his glory: And before him shall be gathered all nations: and he shall separate them one from another, as a shepherd divided his sheep from the goats: And he shall set the sheep on his right hand, but the goats on the left. Then shall the King say unto them on his right hand, Come, ye blessed of my Father, inherit the kingdom prepared for you from the foundation of the world: For I was a hungered, and ye gave me meat: I was thirsty, and ye gave me drink: I was a stranger, and ye took me in Naked, and ye clothed me: I was sick, and ye visited me: I was in prison, and ye came unto me. Then shall the righteous answer him, saying, Lord, when saw we thee an hungered, and fed thee? Or thirsty, and gave thee drink? When saw we thee a stranger, and took thee in? Or naked, and clothed thee? Or when saw we thee sick, or in prison, and came unto thee? And the King shall answer and say unto them, Verily I say unto you, in as much as ye have done it unto one of the least of these my brethren, ye have done it unto me. (31-40).

News flash
Alarming facts about how the poor and needy are perceived by society

Subsequently, the upcoming articles will explain how homeless men and women are really treated by elected Mayors, Commissioners, neighbors as well as those who care about them (advocates). In the article titled, "Homelessness is declining" authors Eric O'Neil, and Jessica Mazzola, wrote based on a survey taken by New Jersey courts. A detailed graph shows that homelessness has decreased in Essex County NJ by 14% since 2014. Essex County Executive Joseph DiVincenzo was quoted in the article with this to say regarding homelessness in Newark, "We still have a profoundly serious problem in Essex County. The economy may have gotten better, but there are still way too many homeless people here." In response to the article "Homelessness is declining," I too agree with this statement, why has not the number of homeless people drop in Newark? James 2 remind us "What doth it profits, my brethren, though a man say he hath faith, and have not works? Can faith save him?" (14). The survey also consists of other counties in New Jersey, and the chart showed Essex County has the largest population of homelessness to be exact 1,723 in comparison to its neighboring counties such as Sussex 57, Salem, Bergen 340 Morris 384, Union 504. I am expressing my thoughts by saying it is a disgrace that Essex County one of New Jersey largest cities is so neglectful of its citizens who are in dire need. Homelessness has risen in Newark, because of lack of concerns, care, and love for the needy; and for our fellow citizens (Star-Ledger June 21, 2015).

James 2

[14] What doth it profits, my brethren, though a man say he hath faith, and have not works? Can faith save him?

[15] If a brother or sister be naked, and destitute of daily food,

[16] And one of you say unto them, depart in peace, be ye warmed and filled; notwithstanding ye give them not those things which are needful to the body; what doth it profits?

I concur that Essex County has far more homelessness issues than the other counties because over the last 15 years, I have seen a vast number of homeless people accumulating at Penn Station Newark, New Jersey. Especially males of diverse background, as well as senior citizens; it breaks my heart to see so many people without a home, especially in the winter. "I asked myself, why?" The authors in "Homelessness declining" also said, many of the other counties were showing a lower percentage of homelessness, because many unsheltered homeless residents were not accounted for because, they were living in cars, parks, and train stations. (Star –Ledger, June 21, 2015). "The count, conducted on Feb.3, found that of the more than 10,000 homeless individuals in the state, 6,934 were staying in emergency shelters, 2,281 were in transitional housing, 974 were unsheltered, and 33 were in safe havens. Each of those figures represents a decrease from last year except the number of unsheltered homeless resident, meaning individuals sleeping in areas such as a car, park, abandoned building or bus or train station the numbers of residents in that category increase slightly from2014, from 931 to 974." Nevertheless, the needy need liberation from the bondage that they are living in; based on the New York Post, issue July 17, 2015, research reveals that New Jersey is not the only state battling with homelessness. Likewise, New York has a severe case of homelessness and they are struggling with how to resolve the problem. In the article titled, "Wake up, de Blasio" author Curtis Liwa, criticize Mayor de Blasio for "running out of excuses and losing touch with reality." "When the Post brought the epidemic of homelessness Hizzoner's he chooses to blame the messengers, lashing out at the Post instead of acknowledging the decaying quality of life in New York City." The Mayor's Department of Homeless Services employees, and police defended him by responding that during, "below freezing temperature the homeless and mentally ill could be forcibly removed from the streets and detained at shelters and hospitals.

To sum it up, the writer's main point in the article is that Mayor de Blasio does not care about the epidemic of homelessness that has occurred in New York City. He gave excuses instead of assisting the mentally ill residents, he seeks to close the very asylum facilities they are supposed to stay in. (New York Post July 17, 2015, nypost.com). Homelessness in New York has gotten so much out of control that citizens are complaining to news anchors.

From my perspective, society has gotten so intolerant of those who are without a home that they do not think one day them or someone close to them may experience homelessness. The majority of those who are affected by homelessness just want someone to love and help them find their way back to normality. Nevertheless, some neighbors turn a blind eye (act has if they don't see the problems) and belittle those who are affected by the homelessness; by calling them "BUMS," The less fortunate are called bums due to their situation and are considered less of a human being because they sleep on the pavement outside without a roof over their head.

From my perspective instead of the neighbors, complaining about the problem with the homeless people, they should get together and introduce themselves to the needy and find how they can assist them. As the Bible rightly says love your neighbor as yourself. Simply put, getting involved, one never knows the difference he or she can make in someone else's life and even possibly bring about a solution. What is even better, one may find out that they too are no different from the individual who is sleeping on the ground.

Likewise, the article titled "It's the new Village people," author Kevin Fasick, wrote about homeless people, who came together and populated a section of Washington Square Park called 1 Greenwich Village after being displaced from Union Square because Christmas- gift stalls were placed there to acknowledge Christmas. However, neighbors were very unhappy with the needy hanging out there and report to the news that the needy were overly aggressive. Inconclusion, a park worker refers to them as "bums" and that the bacilli just litter the place and it was disgracing their community. According to the article, another park worker said the bums "leave their junk everywhere-beer bottles, empty bottles of alcohol, you name it" (pg. 8).

Finally, in the article written by author Priscilla DeGregory titled "The Bums Out," Police commissioner Bill Bratton disagree with the residents giving money to beggars who are sitting outside on the sidewalk with their pets. He thinks residents are only promoting beggars by aiding them. One of the residents implies she gave the money to help the beggar get a sandwich to eat. Another resident stated that these are real people, who are homeless and needs help, which totally disagree with the commissioner's statement. Being an advocate for the poor and needy I disagreed with him. He can help the needy; and not look down on them. He should use his authority to help implement changes to help them rather than preventing others from giving to them. In short, the reason the resident was so kind on this particular day was because they wanted to show compassion to those who were without food and clothes despite what the commissioner of New York have to say. In this quote, a resident says, "She said Bratton's call to stop giving money is "ignoring the situation." "That's it" That's the answer" How does that help this person? This is a real situation. We have homeless people, and they have animals, and they need help," she said. (pg. 5 Shawn Cohen, Kathleen Culliton and Bruce Golding.) I agree with the resident in giving to those in need, because the Bible remind us that "If a brother or sister be naked, and destitute of daily food, And one of you say unto them, depart in peace, be ye warmed and filled; notwithstanding ye give them not those things which are needful to the body; what doth it profits?"(James 2, 15-16).

Nonetheless, one of the most intriguing articles I have read on homelessness was one titled, "This guy was a Wall St. big," by Shawn Cohen, Kathleen Culliton, and Bruce Golding; The article spoke of a man named Preston King, who was once a Wall street high-roller with a prestigious occupation, as a stockbroker and lived the high life in the 1980's. However, he became hooked on drugs, and lost his wealth and was later discover on the streets of New York among the homeless and sleeping on pizza boxes for his bed. He was called a snoozing bum, sleeping with the rat when he was identified by his sister Kristine who looked for him with NYPD Sgt. Paul Capotosto in Washington Square Park.

In conclusion, according to North Jersey.com article titled "'Homeless Epidemic," the city of Clifton is having a big homeless epidemic. Immigrants from countries such as Mexico, Honduras, and Argentina are camping out under the Ackerman Avenue Bridge. These men are not just sitting around doing nothing the article states, it is a squalid place, home to more than a dozen homeless people who retreat there each night after seeking construction work by day." One may ask what the city of Clifton is doing about this crisis, Clifton mentioned they are going to relocate the needy to shelters. It is obvious that homelessness is dominating cities across New Jersey (United States).

Accordenly, homelessness affects all nationalities, and it reminds me of the Civil Right Movement which was led by Dr. Martin Luther King, which occurred during the 50s and late 60s. Dr. King fought for the rights of his people as well as for all other nationalities. He wanted justice for his 4 black children, who were growing up in a white America without the same opportunity as other white children. Furthermore, he marched for the right to integrated schools, restaurants, and the list goes on; black was not allowed to eat in the same restaurants as whites. Unfortunately, they were even denied the privilege go to the same schools, drink from the same water fountain, live in the same community and were deprived of a proper college education. Blacks were refused proper jobs although they were qualified.

Besides, why are we still facing many of these issues? Did not, Dr. Martin Luther King fought so hard for Civil Rights. Moreover, why is homelessness so evident in our society? How can we fix homelessness in our community on a local level and federal level)? CHURCHES MUST GET INVOLVED AS WELL AS MAYORS, ALL ELECTED OFFICIALS LEADERS OF OUR COMMUNITIES AND STATES.

WHAT CAN YOU DO AS A CONCERN AND CARING CITIZEN TO HELP THE NEEDY IN YOUR COMMUNITY?
DO YOU KNOW ANYONE WHO IS HOMELESS?

HOW DID YOU RESPOND TO THEM UPON YOUR FIRST ENCOUNTER?

READERS NOTES

THESE ARE JUST A FEW OFTHE FACES OF THE POOR AND NEEDY LIVING AT NEWARK PENN STATION,

PENN. STATION

NEWARK

Reflections
Pictures of poor and needy

JUST A SAMPLE MEAL OF WHAT IS OFFERED TO THE LESS FORTUNATE AT NEWARK PENN STATION.

L
I
V
I
N
G

I
N

T
H
E

S
T
R
E
E
T
S

O
F

N
E

xxxiv

WARK

NEW

JERSEY

IS

NO

PICNIC

FOR

THE

XXXV

P
O
O
R

A
N
D

N
E
E
D
Y
!

MY BELOVED FRIEND

IN MEMORY OF THE LATE

JEAN

INTRODUCTION

How God Called Me to Help the Poor and Needy

It was late one night in a vision, after I became a Christian the Lord spoke: while I was in bed sleeping. And said, what are you going to do about it? God was referring to feeding His sheep (the needy). The homeless residents, who sleep in dark alleys, cardboard boxes on the sidewalk, and those who sleep at the bus stop. Under bridges, and at bus terminals behind Penn Station, Newark and anywhere they could find to rest their weary heads. I was fearful, and surprise to hear His voice and lay still in bed and listened. I had to be sure it was not my imagination. At that precise moment, it became real with all the passion that was placed inside of me to help the needy from childhood into adulthood had been Gods will for me. He has been showing me them throughout the city of Newark, New Jersey largely streets like Springfield Avenue Mulberry street, Broad Street, Market Street, and Ferry.

It was as if I was conscious yet unconscious, I felt fearful to know the true and living God was speaking to me. Who am I for Him to be speaking to this early in the morning? I did not respond aloud but in my heart, I whispered I will go. The message the Lord gave reminded me of Isaiah the prophet, when God asked, "Who will go?" and he responded, "Send me." Like Isaiah, I felt unworthy and unclean to hear the voice of God? God gave me this word to say to His people, has I hand out the meals, and hugged them. "Jesus loves you." "And I love you too." After the shock, of hearing God's voice. I was thrilled and honored to aid the poor and needy in my neighborhood. The simple message God gave me to tell His people was "Jesus loves you" which kept me passionate and devoted to my task. Although I was excited, it was very alarming sight for me, just looking at people in that condition, and the smell of stale urine, and the loneliness in their eyes. Although God gave me a compassionate spirit towards them, I did not have the guts to approach one face to face, because I did not know their mental state of mind. I took these things into consideration instead of depending on my wisdom, God gave me His way on how to approach them. By placing me on fasting and consecration every time I went to visit them.

Overall, I had to follow the plan the Lord Almighty had for my life which was to pray with the poor and needy, for deliverance, and healing besides feeding them. Therefore, "my answer was yes Lord because I love Him and desire to please Him." I have learned from experience that faith without works is dead. James 2: 14-17 states:

> What doth it profits, my brethren, though a man says he hath faith and have not worked? Can faith save him? If a brother or sister be naked, and destitute of daily food, And one of you say unto them, depart in peace, be ye warmed and filled; notwithstanding ye give them not those things which are needful to the body; what doth it profits? Even so, faith, if it hath not works, is dead, being alone (Gateway Bible.com).

God require me not to only read His word but be a doer by feeding my brothers and sisters on the street. I am delighted when I fulfill God's commandments.

All things consider, this call to ministry was not a surprise for me. As a child growing up in Jamaica, I always had a desire to help people. Even when I migrated to the United States my heart always has a burning ache to help others. Yet, I did not have the courage to do so on my own. Some example of my passions was to help the elderly across the street and carry their groceries. As well as give food to the needy, and money, whenever I see them at Penn Station, or generally in my community. However, I did not have the courage to step out of my comfort zone and do it. I often wondered how they would react and what they would say to me if I approached them. To be honest I was scared to confront them. Thank God for the scripture in the Bible that says, "Be not forgetful to entertain strangers: for thereby some have entertained angels unaware." (Hebrew13:2) This allows me to see that although one looks like a stranger, in the eyes of God they are angels. In fact, who knows God Himself just may be among them. Like when God visit Abraham, in Sodom and Gomorrah 2 angels escorted God down to earth. They inform Abraham of Gods plans to destroy Sodom because of the wickedness of the people as come up to Him. God was indeed one of the 3 angels who went and saw Abraham in Sodom. The Bible says, Abraham ran and bow down before them and brought them in his tent. He gave them water and wash their feet. He fed God and the 2 angels. Then God said I am leaving now. But on His way, God said I cannot hide this thing from my friend Abraham. Apparently, Abraham got the secret of Gods heart. He fed God. If you feed God, He will disclose His secrets to you. Besides, the Bible say the secret of the Lord is with those who fear Him. You feed Him by praising and worshiping.

Last but not least, I looked forward to assisting the needy because it brought joy to my soul. I also cried a lot and asked God to send help from other ministries to help. I thank God for due order in my life which allows me to carry out ministry. Above all, I had to inquire of the Lord for direction about how He desire for me to perform His tasks daily in ministry. Without due order in my life, I would not have been able to accept correction when I make mistakes in ministerial service. Which make it possible for me to continue until now? "Due order." As mentioned in,

> 1 Chronicles 15:11-13:
> And David called for Zadok and Abiathar the priests, and for the Levites, for Uriel, Isaiah, Joel, Shemaiah, Eliel, Amminadab, 12 And said unto them, Ye are the chief of the fathers of the Levites: sanctify yourselves, both ye and your brethren, that ye may bring up the ark of the LORD God of Israel unto the place that I have prepared for it.
>
> For because ye did it not at the first, the LORD our God made a breach upon us, for that we sought him not after the due order. So, the priests and the Levites sanctified themselves to bring up the ark of the LORD God of Israel" (BibleGateway. com).

Like king David, even though we fail at times to seek God for His divine instruction when we realized our mistake we can repent and asked God for His forgiveness. God desire us to perform service with a prescribed method of Due Order. It is only by God's divine grace, favor, and mercies why I am still standing today. Similarly, to Paul the apostle, I can honestly say having obtained favor from the Lord, I continue to this day. Thank God, he has equipped and sustained me during persecution, difficulties, and adversities in the ministry.

> Acts 26 states
> "Having therefore obtain help of God, I continued until this day, witnessing both to and small great, saying none other thing than those which the prophets and Moses say should come: That Christ should suffer, and that he should be the first that should rise from the dead and should show light unto the people and to the Gentiles" (22, 23).

CHAPTER 1

My first Day out in the Field
9/1/14 6:19 p.m.

On my first trip to feed the needy, the Lord led me to Broad Street Newark to hand out sandwiches which; I had prepared at home. Particularly, after my conversion, God used an encouraging message preached by an Apostle in New York City, about faith, and numerous songs on the radio pertaining to radical faith for me to make this bold decision to leave my job. Furthermore, I need to walk by faith and not by sight. In fact, I felt God calling me to leave the job and seek Him further. I was working as a nanny in Fanwood New Jersey. But the family did not appreciate my service, they would come home late every evening with an excuse, but I was expected to be on time for work. Besides, they refuse to pay my social security benefits although I was a permanent resident of the United States. So, I left my job after baptism in Jesus name where I worked for five years because I was very unhappy there. Therefore, I did not know what to expect or what would occur later in my life. However, because of my newfound faith in the Lord, I was excited and did whatever it takes to pursue God. I practice faith, like a baby who was just learning to walk. Thus, began my Christian journey of faith in Christ, leaving one's safe haven and going out in an unfamiliar territory was difficult. As mentioned in the dedication, for sure I was terrified to approach the less fortunate people in need, because of their appearances. Most had on torn old dirty clothes that smelled like urine. Overall, when I first smelled them, I wanted to run. How could I possibly tolerate such odor? Yet, the anointing on my life lifts a standard for me to see what God was showing me. Which was souls for His kingdom. The looks in their eyes reminded me of wild animals, who was lost and desperately in need of affection which made me sad. Inconclusion, something was lacking in their lives deeper than the basic need for food and clothing. And it was love. However, not everyone looked this way just some of them.

> Romans 8
>
> "But God demonstrate his own love for us in this: while we were still sinners Christ died for us."

I suppose after being homeless for a while it took a toll on some of them mentally, and they seem not to care much about their personal hygiene. Or perhaps they cannot find any clean facilities that would allow them to take a shower. As I moved down the street, inside my heart was beating fast, yet for some unknown reason; I was being nudged, and pushed, by the Holy Ghost. Towards a man eating out of the garbage can. Indeed, the Holy Ghost is wise; He knows how to get your attention and develop your courage. What a sight! "It was inhumane to watch another human being eating out of the garbage can in *America*!" I admit I have seen it from afar while riding on the bus, or across the street. But up close it was breathtaking and heartbreaking. That is when I realized I had to get out of myself and do as God told me. It was not about me, God wanted to work through me; by teaching me compassion, and birthing purpose out of my life. As I give a meal to the man eating out of the garbage can." Besides, it appears to me he was "**God's Angel in Disguise**". Furthermore, he grabs the bag out of my hand quickly, as if I were going to harm him. Startled by his expression, I JUMP BACK. How ridiculous, it was for me to think he would have harmed me. Why was I fearful? God knew best and would not have sent me to feed him. He was just "**God's Angel in Disguise**" hungry and needed someone to care, love, and feed him.

On the other hand, some of the people were so used to eating out of the garbage cans that they did not trust anyone. For the fear that, they were terrified to come close to another human or take the food. It is as if they were wrapped up in their own world even though they are in society. The thought of them rejecting food made me so sad. I was not sure of the reason for them not accepting food, I could only speculate at the time that maybe it was; because they were often abused physically, emotionally, and verbally by others who don't value human lives. Perhaps it was because they were viewed in such a negative light, that is was hard for them to trust and confide in their fellow human beings, who have not shown them kindness in the past. Moreover, for everyone that rejects the meal, someone else took it. Like in the days of JESUS'S ministry, He loves and welcomes the poor and needy; His love and sincerity brought about change and so it was for me. Likewise, I was honored, and happy to be chosen by God, to help my fellow man and women in need. Yet, what strikes me the most was the way the people respond to being a help. I have never been so pleased in all my life to assist people who were so thankful; their smiles would brighten my day. Yet, it always troubles me that they had no homes, jobs, and their problems were still unresolved. This problem would lead me into deeper intercessory prayers for the needs of the needy. God did send help from other ministries such as Bloomfield, Parsippany, Edison, New York, and others from Newark. Thus, they too assist the needy with food and other donations. Thank God, they have been feeding the poor and needy consistently as well. In fact, I am truly thankful to God, that I could encounter the other ministries.

At times, I would face adversities as well as rejections on my mission. For instance, while on my journey, I asked a woman if she needs a meal and she cursed. At first, I felt so bad, and thought all she had to say was no. Nonetheless, I said what do I really have to complain about Jesus was spat on for me.

Matthew 26:67 reads, "Then did they spit in his face, and buffeted him; and (Matthew 26:67). Definitely, I was determine not to let insults stop me from pursuing my assignment. Eventually, that day after feeding the needy, God gave me a deeper sense of compassion, love, and devotion for them. Besides, I could not only see, why God was so concern for His children and their wellbeing, in fact I felt what God was feeling for His children. Their hurt, pain, anguish, sickness, their addiction, loneliness, and desire to be accepted into society. Sincerely, he as seen their suffering, like the children of Israel when they were in bondage in Egypt and needed deliverance; their desire was to be recognized as human beings and be treated as such. According to Exodus 12, "Therefore they set task masters over them to afflict them with heavy burdens. They built for Pharaoh stores cities, Pithom and Raamses. But the more they were oppressed, they more they multiplied and the more they spread abroad" (Exodus 12:11-12). Moreover, I love them even more, 'and poured out my heart to the Lord about their needs and inquire about the saving of their souls.

Accordingly, while on the mission field, I face many adversaries and the police were one of them. As I wrote in my "VOLUME 1 HOW GOD USED ME IN AN EXTRAORDINARY AND MIRACULOUS WAYS TO BLESS OTHERS" "To God Be the Glory." For many years, I did have a good relationship with many of the police officer who worked at Newark, Penn Station. In fact, we even spoke, and they encourage me in assisting the poor and needy. Likewise, I too witness to them about the love of God. However, in recent years, there has been a changed, and I was told by a police officer that I could not feed the needy inside Penn. Station. Of course, this was not the same officers, I was affiliated with, so I asked why not, what has changed, and he was very disrespectful towards me. And said, "you can't feed them inside so I began to call my children out of Penn Station, and have them line up outside, and feed them this too became a problem for the offices and they harassed me often and even said," Do you want to go to jail?" "I said don't you know that one day you may become homeless too." If it were one of your family members how would you like them to be treated." "Or worst what if it were you?" This harassment went on for years. Finally, one day I told them I was a Criminal Justice major, they were so surprised. Nevertheless, this did not stop the harassment. During this ordeal, God blessed me with an article about another Christian person in another state who was facing the same issue I was having with the police. I realize immediately, it was a spiritual warfare, I was dealing with in ministry. Often it would leave me, discourage, and not wanting to return to assist the poor. I knew Satan's purpose was to intimidate me and stop me from my mission God as called me to do. With this in mind, I had to do what God told me to do and keep feeding the needy. Even when I told God, I was not going back to Penn. Station. He would send the needy to me while driving in my car or on the streets, they would just approach me. God allowed saints to call me with prepare food to feed the needy. Eventually, I returned and fed the needy.

One evening a police officer told me to go across the street and not to feed them on New Jersey Transit property. Some of my children say just go over there and I went. I often prayed about it and told God about my problems. Another incident occurred one evening while I was inside Penn Station handing out tracks two officers came to me and said we had to leave. I told them I have been handing out Bible tracks for 13 years at Penn Station, and they said "No you are not allowed to do that here I insisted on knowing why and asked him who was his supervisor. I asked for their names as well. Again, I was at Penn Station one evening and two officers came and told me and my friend we had to leave, and I asked why, and he said you are not allowed to hand out those here. Like the officers before, I told them it been 13 years I have been here doing this and no one has stop me before in fact the other officer I met were exceedingly kind to me. I insisted on knowing why the change and I refused to leave. Finally, I told them I need to speak with their superior, because I knew God was with me and fighting my battle immediately HE STARTED to turn me around in the spirit and "told me to ask them if they believed in God, "one of the officers said I do." "I go to church," I asked him, where and he told me, White Plains New Jersey. "I said to him how can you stop us from handing out tracks if you say that you are a Christian?" He did not know what to say; instead. He just stared at me for a moment with a confused look on his face. Finally, he told me to go to New Jersey Transit and asked for a permit. He points me in the direction of the office, which was to the far left of track 4. Upon going there, the customer service personnel, told me he never heard of such a thing. There were no permits given to hand out Bible literature. I realized this person was also a Christian. I when back to the officer and told him what the gentleman said. He gave me another address of a building outside Penn Station, Newark and told me to inquire there. In a few days, I was there and got some information from a Hispanic lady name Rosa who help me. Although I never met her in person, I told her what had occurred and she gave me, a permit. It has been 7 years now. I am still on the mission field for Jesus. In addition, to these occurrences in 2012 I was given a name and a number to call by a white officer regarding handing out tracks. When I called the number, the individual on the phone told me there were no such permits given out to hand out track just to negate it. He said, I was free to hand out the tracks, and he did not know why the police officer told me that. I never let the devil stop me, when God says, "go." I go!" When he says move, "I move." Whatever, God tells me to do I will, and shall not be afraid of their faces. However, I realized that God was working out His plan for my life and all I had to do was be obedient. As the word of God says, and we know that all things work together for our good to those who love God to those who are the called according to His purpose" (Romans 8:28).

We are all God's creation, and we are here to help each other. Certainly, it is not difficult, to see the needs of others around us. In fact, it is so evident in our society that there are hurting, hungry people around us the differences are we willing to assist them when it is in our power to help? Does it take a whole lot to impact someone's lives? All one must do is try. It occurred to me that although, I was not rich God has given me the ability to think and find ways to assist the needy, whether it was in small or large quantity. Like Jesus who used 2 fish and five loaves of bread to feed the multitude.

According to Gateway Matthew14

And Jesus went forth, and saw a great multitude, and was moved with compassion toward them, and he healed their sick. And when it was evening, his disciples came to him, saying, this is a desert place, and the time is now past; send the multitude away, that they may go into the villages, and buy themselves victuals. But Jesus said unto them, they need not depart; give ye them to eat. And they say unto him, we have here but five loaves, and two fishes. He said, bring them hither to me. And he commanded the multitude to sit down on the grass and took the five loaves, and the two fishes, and looking up to heaven, he blessed, and brake, and gave the loaves to his disciples, and the disciples to the multitude. And they did all eat and were filled: and they took up of the fragments that remained twelve baskets full. And they that had eaten were about five thousand men, beside women and children. (6-21)

Subsequently, it really does not matter when one is hungry whether they are given a lavish meal, or not. Besides, as one can see all that Jesus had was five loafs of bread, and two fishes. He was moved with compassion for the multitude and He bless it and gave it to them. Hence the gift of love certainly works wonders when it is put into action. Jesus exemplifies it here when He prayed to His Father with His whole heart and the food was multiply. Accordingly, it is for us today that whatever one can afford to give to the less fortunate (From the heart) they will except it. Especially if one cannot afford it, what really makes a difference to the person in need is a caring soul who comes along; and offer all they have with love. The response is always the same for me, one of gratitude. I found out that a hungry and hurting person never complain about the food given to them they, readily accept whatever, is given to them with love. Likewise, this appreciation helps me to continue to help others, who are in need. In short, I take great pleasure in giving to others. My goal is to be liked my Father Jesus. It is my greatest desire to be like Jesus while living on this earth and accomplish all He had as well as exceeded Him. Accordingly, the Bible says, John 14:12 "Truly, truly, I say unto you, he that believes in me, the works that I do that shall he also do ;and greater works than these shall he do; because I go unto my father.(John 14) No one knows who they really are until they follow Christ. Hence the Bible says, "These signs shall follow them that believe; In my name they shall cast out devils; they shall speak with new tongues" (Mark 16 :17-18).

CHAPTER 2

I know Jesus Came Himself Just For Me in the Form of an Ark Angel.

January 19/17 5:00 p.m

All I knew was that God had heard my heart's cry for the past two weeks. He had it all planned, how He would bless me. Furthermore, I had no clue that today was my day of healing and deliverance. Throughout the past months I have been going through heartaches, stress and sleep deprive, because the new tenant's living downstairs have been keeping me up on weekend with wild parties. My landlady does not seem to care. I had to call 911 which in turn told me to call the Newark police department. Therefore, the police were called to our place of residence at mid-night and 2 a.m. in the morning at numerous times. I often prayed and followed all the instruction God gave, which led up to the police coming one night when for instance I called and the tenants ran out the house, when they came and hide. Besides, they often had loud fights too. My prayer was for God to move me out the house or they had to go but I could not live with them there. God had not opened the opportunity for me to move and He had not allowed them to relocate either. Overall, I got to the point where I made certain comments to God about how I feel. Certainly, I did not hide my feelings from Him, because I was also facing other physical issues. So, I asked God for a special gift; just to determine if He was hearing my prayers. Simultaneously, the waiting process was difficult. How long did God want me to wait before my petition was granted? It was such a piece of cake so to speak. In brief, I thought it was an easy task for God because He is love. To put it briefly, according to scripture God's thoughts are not our thoughts. Isaiah 55:8, 9 states, "For my thoughts are not your thoughts neither are my ways," declare the Lord. As the heavens are higher than

> Matthew 22:39
>
> The second is "like namely this, thou shalt love thy neighbor as thyself, There is no other command greater than these."

the earth, so are my thoughts than your thoughts" (Isaiah). Lastly, God commanded us to love one another and it is lacking even among us believers. To sum it up, I questioned God one day and asked: "who would be my, **Angel In Disguise**" to bless me. If people could read my mind as I passed, them on the streets searching strange face to glimpse if Jesus was there. Nevertheless, I guess one is so wrapped up in one's own problems that even if God spoke to an individual; they are not sensitive to the voice of God, to yield to His prompting in one's heart. Likewise, family members were busy with the cares of life. So, I did not find the answer there. Consequently, they were not the ones God chosen to carry out His assignment. Similarly, church members did not know my heart's request either and most of them only shake your hand. If they knew of my needs, it would have been granted. Therefore, I kept on asking the Sovereign God, "When will He grant me my little itty-bitty prayer request. In the meantime, my heart was aching just for that special touch. Initially, as I continue to serve in ministry and the days go by, I became more hopeful for the manifestation of my desire. To the point, where I go up to people and smile in their faces to see if they were the one God selected to grant me, my special gift. Thus, I know it sounds crazy but that was my expectation. Yet, each time it was hopeless," they would only smile back and say how are you doing." And moved on, or a simple handshake? One of the reasons for asking God for the request, was because of issues I was facing, financial problems which seemed endless. In contrast, I was going through so many hard times and need just a simple thing from God that could release some of the pressure out of my life. These circumstances led up to me feeling discouraged. In the hope that it would relieve most of the problems, but if was so scarce among God's people. All those I have extended myself to help or prayed for had abandon me. Given these facts, whether I asked God for something or He promises me a gift, I will go to the ends of the earth to retrieve it. Therefore, what happened this Sunday morning at GLC was a mind blower, God was waiting for me to show up at church that glorious Sunday morning. To summarize, our ministry is special because it's not like one of those mega-churches, on the contrary, everyone knows each other in our assembly. It has a lovely white cross on it with a radiant light when the sun shines on it. While at church I reflected on my prayer. I was specific and adamant about my request it was so simple, yet it seems as if God would not grant me it. But I knew, He would not deny me, "Because He said in His word you asked anything in His name it shall be done." John 14:13, 14 "And I will do it whatever you ask in my name, so that the Father may be glorified in the son. You may ask me anything in my name, and I will do" (John). Lastly, as I settle down in the front seat of our congregation, my attention was not focused on my special request that day. With this in mind, I am not even clear why I attended church that morning because my burden was so heavy form lack of sleep. It is exceedingly difficult for me to worship God when I am over tired. Moreover, I always tell the Lord, He deserves the best, and being happy inside out as I worship God is very vital to me. Furthermore, I don't want to be fake because God knows my heart. As the Bible says, "God is a spirit and they that worship Him must worship Him in spirit and in truth." Thus, I was lacking sleep, because my neighbors on the 1st floor played loud music all night and did not turn it off until 2 a.m. Although, I called the Newark, police department again to complain about the horrible noise, but after they left the premises my neighbor turn back up the music. All I knew was that I LOVE the Lord and I am crazy about Him. Therefore, that's always my reason for going to church. At times, life problems would impact my life so much that it tries to shift my faithfulness to God as promised on the day of water baptism to serve Him for the rest of my life. Although, I know to reach heaven there must be faithfulness until death. That morning, I had chosen a bright yellow suit to wear to church to brighten my day and lift my spirit. What's more I had learned through the power of the Holy Ghost that under all circumstances of my life I must worship God, because that is why He created me. And the devil will not get God's glory. In addition, I was not about to stay home and sleep or have a pity party, God deserves better than that. Indeed, God is awesome mighty, and no respecter of person. The incredible God showed up that afternoon in the church. He disguised Himself as one of my children and gave me a hugged that healed my broken heart. It happened after worshipped service was over the moderator came to the pulpit and said give someone a hug. 'What! I was surprise God had revealed my request in church." Furthermore, coming in late to service, I had noticed a tall dark stranger sitting across the aisle on the other side. In fact, I looked across at her and knew I had never seemed her before. For some reason, my heart goes out to her. She was about four hundred pounds the size of a giant and dress in shabby bright orange and red clothing. She walked over to me smiling. At once, I smell a familiar smell (she was homeless) and gave me the biggest hugged I ever experience in my life. As **"God's Angel In Disguise,"** embrace me, it felt like she was squeezing the life out of me. But "I love it." Particularly, she took a long time before she releases me. Indeed, I felt like heaven came down and glory filled my soul. No doubt, it was a good laugh for me; here I was expecting a hugged from those nearest and dearest to me. Hence, God gave me what and who He knew was best for me and He was right. Throughout serving God, He has often, brought people in angelic form to hug me, in my times of loneliness. Therefore, I laugh because they go as quickly as they come in a flash. Needless to say, these occurrences would brighten my day, and nights, which reminded me that God was with me and loves and care about me. These assurances are never too much when I was going through personal issues, but this one exceeds them all. In the past, God as used children, youths, and seniors to bless my heart. Overall, God would send me love wrapped up in His children's. He is so radically and crazy in love with me. I really could not get over this blessing, God as disguised Himself as a homeless woman, "Just for me!" I could not ask for anything more. Without a word, she walks away. I was stunned! "It was great!" "Just what I had been waiting for the past months God had granted me the desire of my heart, no money, gold,or silver in the world could have lighten my burdens and bless my heart as this gift. Yes, it was the precious anointing of God, it will forever be with me till I die. God always knows how to make me laugh, I concluded that I did not know Him at all. Because when I think to know Him, He often time comes in another form and size. God is GOOD TO ME. After which she walked out of the sanctuary never to be seen again. The mistake I made was hesitating to follow her. At the time, it looked like she was heading downstairs towards the restroom, but instead, she exited the building. Initially, I wanted to run after her to find out who she was, and if I could be of assistant to her. To this day I, which I have, pursued her. As the Bible says, entertain strangers because you may entertain angels unaware Hebrews 13:2 states, "Be not forgetful to entertain strangers: for thereby some have entertained angels unawares" (Hebrews). God made himself conspicuously that day, by appearing as **An Angel in Disguise,** through the homeless woman. As the Bible reminded us that God as assigned one or more angels to those who are save for their protection. Angels are available to people who are saved or people who will be saved. Matthew 18: 10 states, "see that you do not despise one of these" little ones for I say to you that their angels in heaven continually behold the face of my Father who is in heaven" (Matthew). Therefore, watch out how you treat God's little children because there are angels, who are assigned to protect them. Similarly, Bible said, angels look in the face of God to hear what God wants them to do with the person who is messing with His precious children. In conclusion, just because you are, one of God's children He will show up on time to bless and help you in the time of need, when you least expect Him and blow your mind.

<u>JESUS IS THE WAY!</u>

CHAPTER 3

My Christmas Boots
September11/14 6:19p.m

As I sat in my 1987 black sports car few days before Christmas. I was beside myself trying to replace my winter boots that were worn out. Dress in my old shabby boots with winter clothing and my favorite furry black hat. Pondering in my heart where to look next for my shiny black boots. Of course, the search for my new boots did not begin on Christmas Eve, but long before that. I had even taken great pleasure to ask the person who had given me the boots where she had purchased them. Nevertheless, she said, "she could not remember where she had gotten them." "Maybe it was at the thrift store." The reason I appreciate those boots so much is that they came up to my knees and were a perfect fit. They allow my legs to stay warm in the snowy wintry days, especially while on the mission field.

All I knew was that I needed a new pair fast, and I could not locate them anywhere within the stores. In fact, my boot heels were crooked, and they were becoming increasingly dangerous for me to walk in without sliding. Each step I took in them was in fact a step of faith. To this day I do not know if it was a good thing to do but when one trust God, they do unusual things. I began to pray and asked the Lord to 'please' guide me to locate them. Besides, I was determined to find them, although my eyes seen a lean pair of boots that could throw me down at any given moment. My spiritual heart believes that God

And he shall set the sheep on his right hand, but the goats on the left.

Then shall the King say unto them on his right hand, Come, ye blessed of my Father, inherit the kingdom prepared for you from the foundation of the world:

For I was an hungred, and ye gave me meat: I was thirsty, and ye gave me drink: I was a stranger, and ye took me in:

Naked, and ye clothed me: I was sick, and ye visited me: I was in prison, and ye came unto me.

would see me through my current problem and provide a new pair for me. I had long decided that I would not let my eyes determine what my heart believed. As God word say speak to the mountains and they shall be removed. I was determined to continue wearing the boots downtown, Newark to feed the needy. I refused to let the condition or shape of my boots hindered me from pursuing my goal.

As a result, I began to search the local stores for them, After all, the Bible says faith without works is dead According to James 2 "Even so faith, if it hath not works, is dead, being alone" I knew God would come through for me if I only trust Him. Realizing these boots could come from any store, in New Jersey, I extended my faith and search. Therefore, I decide in my heart to pray again and let the Lord lead me to the stores that sold them. Is there anything too hard for God when one believes? (James 2).

Finally, on Christmas Eve, one evening while on my way home, I realized the Lord was prompting me to check two stores on route 22 East, across from Red Lobster. This was thrilling because I was determined to bless myself with those boots as a Christmas gift. Isaiah 65:16 says " That he who blesses himself in the earth shall bless himself in the god of truth; and he that swearth in the earth shall swear by the god of truth; because the former troubles are forgotten, and because they are hid from mine eyes" . The first store I checked was Wal-Mart and the store were very festive with Christmas carols playing. The lines to the cash register were extremely long. The store aisles were packed like sardines with last minute Christmas shoppers. Some customers hands were full of gifts and children tugging along behind them. Quickly, but carefully, I check the boots section and the end results was that they did not have them. It seems as if I was not making any progress. Next, I tried K-mart and it was even more crowded with Christmas shoppers. The store looked like a tornado had passed through it, because boots were scattered all over the isles and on the benches. But after a diligent search, I found the boots. I began to jump up and down in the store with excitement, just grateful to the Lord. Eventually, I began to search frantically with great expectation for my size, but unfortunately, they were all sold out of my size. The only sizes remaining were a miss match a size 8 and an 8 ½. And I wore a size 8 ½. However, I did not give up! A winner never quit, and you can't keep a woman of God down. l kept on searching for the other match to the size 8 ½ and did not find it. But for some reason, I could not stop searching.

Finally, I said, "Lord I don't believe you brought me this far, and I still cannot find my "special boots." After all this is not OJ's trial when the gloves did not fit. I am a child of God. "Still not ready to quit." With great anticipation, I asked a smiling salesperson to help me search for my size. Regrettably, we did not find it. For a moment, I feel like a child whose heart was broken and wanted to cry." "Why did the Lord brought me here if He knew the boots didn't match? "I did not want to leave the store empty handed without my boots. "I couldn't understand it. "Was this a joke or a test of my faith, "I asked myself?" Similarly, Sarah and Abraham when faced with a promised God had told them that they would have a child in their old age. They thought it was impossible due to the barrenness of Sarah's womb and Abraham being 100 years old. According to the Bible, "For Sarah conceived, and bore Abraham a son in his old age, at the set time of which God had spoken to him." (Genesis 21:2) "Did God want to see how I would react, if He did not grant me my heart's desire just this once by not allowing me to find my special boots?" "And if I would let it damper my spirit and hinder me from assisting the needy tomorrow, Christmas Day? That night, I left the store with my head hanged low as I walked out very slowly, I pondered the entire issue in my heart. By the time, I reached the parking lot my faith picked up again. The anointing of God was present, and it made me laugh. Although I did not find my boots, I was still determined to feed my children the next day (Christmas) in my black crooked old boots. As the old saying goes," you can't keep a good woman down." New boots, or old boots I did not know what God was up to, but I still had a mission to accomplish with His help.

Christmas Eve night was an exciting time for me. Although I had just gotten home from work, I was not tired. In fact, I felt super charged and energized by the Holy Ghost to hand out the gifts to the needy in my community. Even though I had not located my boots, I did not let that bother me, I had hopes that it would all work out simply fine. My main concern was to deliver the Christmas gifts to the needy. Once downtown Newark, and loaded the packages into my cart, I noticed there was a shift in the temperature outside and it was colder and windier. I pulled my coat tighter around my neck to keep warm. As I hurried along the busy street, many passersby were rushing by perhaps doing their final Christmas shopping and heading towards the train to visit their loved ones. Within minutes, I was in my usual location, but I did not see my special friend who always helped me bless the needy. This concerned me, as I began to serve the people who were online to receive their gift. I hugged each one, and said "Merry Christmas," as I handed them their gifts. In a matter of minutes all the gifts were gone, everyone appreciates his or her present.

Nonetheless, I was not in a hurry to go home because I was still looking for my friend. His name is James. He is a slender African American in his mid-50s, with his front teeth missing. But love to smile a lot. He too was homeless at times, moving from one shelter to another. Also, he was given an apartment with the aid of section 8 (Governments program that aid underprivileged people with their rent). He has such a kind heart. He was one of the first homeless man which I encountered while assisting the needy at Newark Penn, Station. He has a desire to help serve others as well. Since I started working downtown, I cannot recall a time when he had not participated in helping me to hand out the meals or gifts. However, tonight of all nights he was missing. "I asked some of the others if they saw him, but they said, "No." This concerned me because we had developed a friendship, and I usually spend time witnessing to him about God. He often put off the subject of rededicating his life to God. I just wanted to make sure that he was ok. I started to inquire of the Lord if he was alright because this was not like James. One of James's good quality was, he took such pleasure in helping others although he too was in need. He always wanted to know what time I would be there just so he could help me hand out the food and call the others to form a line.

As I ponder it in my heart about what could have happened to James. I began to reminisce on the past summer, and how God had used him at one point to bless my life. Since God delivered me from high blood pressure 15 years ago. Aside from bananas, one of my favorite snacks was peanuts. However, I noticed that eating too many salty peanuts, was not good for my health, and decided to eat unsalted peanuts instead. Switching from a bad habit to a good habit was not easy. However, it must have pleased the Lord because ironically, he uses James to bless me with unsalted peanuts one afternoon after I fed the needy.

As we walked towards the newspaper stand at the corner of Market Street, at the traffic light. James told me to go and asked the owner for a bag of peanuts, and "I said no!" "He laughs." "I thought it was a joke at first." "But he insisted." And "Call out to the owner." I felt a bit uncomfortable because there were so many people standing around waiting by the newspaper stand for their buses. What was he doing, I did not want him to spend any money on me. I never told James about peanuts being one of my favorite snacks. It seems as if God had revealed my thoughts to him, as we reached the stand, "He began to explain that he had been working there for some time now, and it was ok." "His boss would take it out of his wages. "I was still uncertain about the whole idea and began to communicate with the Lord in my heart when the owner interrupted me and confirmed his story. "He too insists I took the peanut." With a thick Pakistan accent and a smile, he said, "Yes take it."

At times, it astonished me because of the simple ways, and people the Lord would use to bless me. "Is there anything too hard for God?" Here it was I was giving James who was in need, and God was using him as well to bless me. God as taught me to take from others because that's how they receive their blessing. As I stood there, in the cool of the night reflecting on God's goodness, I SUDDENLY LOOKED UP TOWARDS THE ENTRANCE OF PENN STATION, AND JAMES WAS COMING OUT THE DOOR VERY HAPPY. I RAN OVER AND HUGGED HIM. I was so happy to see him and he was laughing. "I asked him where he have been." He just smiles, and "handed me a large bag." "I was surprised; I was not expecting anything from him." "He insisted I opened it right away." I felt a bit embarrassed because the others were watching me. Then out of curiosity, I said ok. I opened the bag, and there was a box, but not just a box but a shoe box. As I pulled out the box, it seemed long and heavy. I could feel the excitement within me growing. When I opened the box, there it was, "MY CHRISTMAS BOOTS!" "THE ONES THAT I HAVE BEEN SEARCHING FOR." "IN MY SIZE AND COLOR." SHINY JET BLACK" "JUST WHAT I WANTED." "IT CAME FROM THE SAME STORE THAT I WAS TRYING TO PURCHASE IT FROM LAST NIGHT." ALL I COULD DO TO RELEASE THE JOY THAT WAS LOCKED UP INSIDE OF ME WAS SHOUT FOR JOY AT THE TOP OF MY LUNGS. IT WAS JUST TOO MUCH FOR ME TO CONTAIN. I put down the box on the payment and began to "JUMP UP AND DOWN." I RAN! I RAN! HOP, SKIP, LAUGH, AND JUMPED SOME MORE. I don't know how my old crooked boots did not throw me down. All I could say was "Thank you, Lord." "YOU

ARE A GOOD GOD" "Thank you for my LOVELY Christmas boots". I KEPT SHOUTING AT THE TOP OF MY LUNGS, "YOU ARE THE SAME GOD YESTERDAY AND TODAY FOREVER THE SAME" "Thank you, Jesus," "FOR MY MIRACLE" "Thank you, James," "James and the others were laughing at me" And, "then with me." "AS BUSY CHRISTMAS SHOPPERS PASS BY, WHO WERE HEADING IN AND OUT OF THE PENN STATION; THEY TOO STOPPED" AND "STARED AT ME WORSHIPPING GOD AND LAUGHED"

I never expected such a wonderful surprise from God. It was hard for me to catch my breath and composed myself. To be honest, I had no pride at all, I just want to bow down on the pavement and worship "My God "because He is so "GOOD TO ME". "GOD HAS AN APPOINTED TIME FOR EVERYTHING IS THERE ANYTHING THING TOO HARD FOR GOD?" I asked myself.

I hugged James and told him my story of how I have been trying to find my boots. I was so grateful to God for sending James, **"God's Angel In Disguise"** I never imagined in my wildest dreams that this could ever happen to me. "How did God pull this one off?" And "Hid it from me?" I usually know when God was up to something big in my life (I feel it in my spirit). God has blessed me to be a problem solver so often I am granted the honor and privilege to figure out what He is up to in my life, through prayer, fasting and a special gift He gave me.

"I kept asking James how he knew my boots size." And "That I needed a pair of boots?" "But the question that bothers my mind was how James was able to purchase my boots?" "I wanted to know how he was able to pay for them because his salary was so meager." As well as, how did he get to the store, because he does not own a car "James just laughed at me as I questioned him?" Well, God must find it amusing and maybe I am just a bit too curious and need to stay out of God's business. God did not reveal His secret to me on how He was able to accomplish this fantastic mission. God ways are far past finding out how he manifests His power and works through a vessel to bring forth His special blessings. I will never forget that night has long as I live. The angelic hand of God was written all over my "CHRISTMAS BOOTS." God as never failed to grant me His desire for my life after fulfilling His service to His people. According to the book of Nehemiah, "Then I told them of the hand of my God which was good upon me; as also the king's words that he had spoken unto me. And they said, let us rise up and build. So, they strengthened their hands for this good work. (2:18).

The Sovereign God showed up in disguise tremendously for me when I was not expecting Him. THANK YOU, LORD, FOR REWARDING ME WITH MY CHRISTMAS BOOTS. God's Angels operate by means of authority and in perfect order. I Corinthian 14 :40 says,' Let all things be done decently and in order" (14:40) "In other words, unless things are operating in an orderly fashion it is not God, because God is not the author of confusion, but a God of order.

CHAPTER 4

"Richard's Blessing to me"

February 11/14 5:00 p.m.
September 2/15 7: p.m
"Richard's Blessing to me"

Agentle summer breeze blow through an open window as the birds chirps softly. I had just stepped out of the shower worshipping and entered my tiny bedroom, which faces the street surrounded by trees. As I got dress, to leave the house and feed the less fortunate. An incredible idea came to my mind to challenge God and make a covenant with Him regarding a book project I was currently working on. I pulled out a big "Poland Spring" water bottle, out of its hiding place, and positioned it in the middle of my small third floor bedroom apartment; then held it up to the Lord in faith, "As I BEGAN TO SPEAK TO HIM THIS TREMENDOUS ANOINTING FELL FROM HEAVEN ON ME." I prophesied and said, "Lord when you bless my first book to be published; I would give this money to charity. Although I had made an investment in the upcoming project already, I just wanted to prove God further, by adding an additional token. Sincerely, enough I was hoping for a vast income from the investment because parts of the earnings were for God's kingdom.

For a moment, I felt like Samson, who God had raised up in the Bible. Who was equipped with this enormous strength to fight the philistines who were constantly at war with the Israelites. He loves

And he shall set the sheep on his right hand, but the goats on the left.

Then shall the King say unto them on his right hand, Come, ye blessed of my Father, inherit the kingdom prepared for you from the foundation of the world:

For I was an hungred, and ye gave me meat: I was thirsty, and ye gave me drink: I was a stranger, and ye took me in:

Naked, and ye clothed me: I was sick, and ye visited me: I was in prison, and ye came unto me.

Delia a Philistine woman desired to marry her. Sampson strength was above is capability and he killed a lion with his bare hands and eat honey from its carcass. Judge 14:8-10 says, "He turned aside to look at the lion's carcass, and in it he saw a swarm of bees and some honey. He scooped out the honey with his hands and ate as he went along. When he rejoined his parents, he gave them some, and they too ate it. But he did not tell them that he had taken the honey from the lion's carcass" (Judges). To top it off, I laugh, because the bottle was so big and heavy. I wanted to put it down but I continued my conversation further with God, and asked, "If He would do me the honor and bless it as a covenant between us to prosper His Kingdom." It contains money, I had collected for years, such as quarters, nickels, pennies, one-dollar bills, five dollars and rear coins.

Overall, this bottle of money has helped me during difficult times. For example, when I was unemployed, and needed money to support myself. I would go to the bottle; it has always been so faithful to me. Not to mention when my car was not working, I had to take the bus and train to work I got my bus fare from it. It was my "rainy day" source. Although, I was grateful for the help, I was not happy when it depleted so quickly. In fact, I vow that as soon as God blessed me with another job, I would invest more money in it. I never wanted to give this bottle of money away because it held sentimental value to me. In essence it was like an old friend, one who does not tell my secrets. Besides, for some crazy reason "call faith", I decide to part with my money bottle, what better way to utilize it, than to give it back to the giver. "Jesus." But I had to use "radical faith" and challenge God. Immediately to find out how much He was paying attention, and listening to me, when I spoke to Him. I knew that if God were truly listening to me and it was His will the manifestation would proceed shortly thereafter. I felt deeply passionate about the idea and know in my heart that my dearly, beloved Papa Jesus, would accept the challenge. He was the one who always initiated the test and challenges in my Christian journey, and I learn to test Him back as well. He does not like for me to lay back on my "gift of faith" but to put it to great use and being, proactive, and conscious of its great purpose in this world if utilize properly. I certainly would not know how far it would take me in God unless I activate it. After all, I have never really challenge God concerning financial matters in such a big way before. It is usually in some other issue, mainly relating to healing. Besides, I was embarking on a new season in my spiritual faith life with God. I was only relaying back to God what He said to me," Which was He had blessed me to "prosper." And it was my, "time to shine." And my "turn to "rise." I just laugh, in the bedroom with God. I knew He would do it for me. No matter what I have always put my trust in God because He believes in me.

From that moment on, I knew my book would publish, although I had not yet signed a contract with a publishing company. It has been years since I have been seeking a good publishing company through prayer and fasting. Although, I have spoken with several book-publishing consultants from publishing companies, I had some issues with them. I had rested the matter for a while, and waited on God, because most of them were dishonest.

However, I know without a doubt that my blessing was on its way because I had great expectation from God. A few months later, a message came from the Lord through a preacher, who preached on the topic "Dig Another Well." It involved Abraham's son, Isaac who refuse to compromise his faith in God. Instead, He focus his attention on what God was telling him to do. He did not fight with the Philistine, but continue to dig wells, and was prosperous even though the Philistines, his enemies were jealous and told him he had to relocate. They did not want him, digging wells close by their land. Finally, God blessed Isaac to dig a well, called "Rehoboth" "God make room." I had decided to try to publish God's book again and He was leading me on a happy and victorious adventure. In short, the preacher helped me to realize that every word, I had spoken had been in extended faith in God, and He was manifesting and bringing forth confirmation in my life.

This well was very instrumental to Isaac and God also prosper Him. Just like Isaac, in the Bible I too refuse to fight with my enemies. The Philistines fought Isaac over the wells he dug. After I prayed in my jeep, I left home happy. It was pack to capacity with meals for the needy, and I was on my merry way singing and rejoicing. It was warm and beautiful outside as I worshiped; and traveled through the neighboring cities. When I reached, my destination downtown Newark, "I felt a shift in the spiritual realm, and I know something good was about to happen." I began to cross at the light heading to my usual location. Then the Lord spoke to my heart to cross over at the other light and go under the bridge. I hesitate for a moment, then proceed. In my heart, I perceived there was someone there who needed a meal. So gladly, I follow the Lord. As I cross over the light and walked beneath the under path, it was crowded with Hispanic American and African Americans people waiting for their buses. As well as those rushing to catch their trains, I could hardly maneuver my cart to get by. Nonetheless, I squeeze through, the numerous groups of people, the noise from the cars, and New Jersey Transit bus were deafening to my ears. Not to mention, the loud conversations that were going on from the commuters, who were standing at the bus stop. It was then that the Lord spoke to me again and got my attention by saying, "There was a man, who was in need there". When I look there was a tall dark young man, and his back was turned towards me. At first glance, one would not think he was in need, because he was well dressed in bright orange colors. That is why it is not good to judge a book by its cover but depend on the Holy Ghost leading to know what is right. I could hear the Lord, "saying he is in need." "I looked at the man." Obviously, God read my thoughts because I began to look around, then back towards the direction I was coming from. It was then I make eye-contact with the dark skin man in the bright orange top. I gaze at the man and express my thoughts to God. I said in my heart, "Lord is he really in need." Until this day, I do not know why I doubt God at that time. Before I could receive the answer from the Lord; the man came rushing over to me frantically, and excited, with a big smile and said, "Yes" it's me "Yes." "Yes" "I am in need." "I am here I need some food." I just looked at him and smiled then repented in my heart to God. Like King David in the Bible, I too tend to ask God when I should pursue an issue or wait.

1 Samuel 1:30, "And David enquired of the LORD, saying, Shall I pursue after this troop? Shall I overtake them? And he answered him, pursue for thou shalt surely overtake them, and without fail recover all. So, David went, he and the six hundred men that were with him, and came to the brook Besor, where those that were left behind stayed" (130: 8- 9). David was devastated after returning from battle with his men and found out that their families was taken, and the city was burnt down. His only option was to turn to the Lord for the answer and God told David to pursue.

I inquire of the Lord if it was the right person, I was about to serve. "And laughed in my heart." Then aloud! Which reminds me of Sara, who laugh when God told her, she would bring forth a son in her old age. Genesis 18 says, Now Abraham and Sarah were old and well stricken in age, and it ceased to be with Sarah after the manner of women. Therefore, Sarah laughed within herself, saying, after I am waxed old shall I have pleasure, my lord being old also? And the LORD said unto Abraham, wherefore did Sarah laugh, saying, Shall I of a surety bear a child, which am old?" (11-13). I thought it was funny how God brings His divine purpose about in our lives. God was one of the 3 angels who went and saw Abraham before the other 2 angels when and visit Lot in Sodom. Abraham ran and brought them in his tent and gave them water to refresh and wash their feet. He also fed them, when God was finish eating, He said I am leaving now but on His way; God said, "I can't hide this thing from my friend Abraham." However, today God will not come down and have dinner with us has He did with our fourth Father Abraham, but He still reveals His secret to us if we worship Him from a sincere heart. The secret of God was revealed to Abraham after he fed God. If one fed God He will disclose His secret to you. Worshipping God daily on a consistent basis is the best way to fed God and have sweet fellowship with Him. Like this man, God did not make mistake in our lives when He bring us together. He was so happy for the food and I was, even more, please to serve him. He asked for seconds without eating the first portion. In essence I did not ask him why I just gave it to him. He was immensely helpful to me and wanted to help me put my cart back together. He looked at me closely, and said, "I know you." And I said, "You do." curiously! "He said yes." I was sure he looked familiar. Nonetheless, I fed so many people it is impossible for me to remember everyone faces or names. He began to remind me that I was there a few weeks ago and one of my assistants fed him a fried chicken meal. He even went as far as to describe her to me. He said, "She wore glasses." And "was dark complexion." I knew who he was talking about she was a college student who typically helped me in the summer. However, she had returned to college. I marveled at God and this young man. Expressively, he was one of "**God's Angel in Disguise.**" Fortunately, for me God does not miss a beat of what His children are doing in His kingdom. At that moment, "I said goodbye." And he said, "Wait." And put his hand in his pocket and pulled out a hand full of change and hand it over it to me. He said, "This is for you." "I said what!" He said, "Yes take it." "" I laugh because I realized it was not him, but God working through him" (I knew it was the angel of the Lord). It must have been a sight to the spectators as the man in need gave me a hand full of change. Finally, I said to him, "I do not have anywhere to put it." Instantly, I remember for the first time in years, I had my backpack on my back. I had forgotten to put it in the jeep as I normally do. But I was too far away, from the jeep to return when I realized my mistake I said, "Lord please forgive me for not returning to put my bag in the jeep." I am custom to leaving it, because there is no accommodation for it when I serve the needy. I PRAYED, and asked the Lord for His protection, as I continue with it on my back. Consequently, that is when it hits me, this was the purpose I had carried my handbag. I thought, "What a joke this must be in heaven to God and His holy archangels God knew all along I would need it for the money." There were so many coins, quarts, dimes, nickels, and pennies. It could barely fit in the zipper side of the handbag. I asked him for his name, and he replied Richard. In brief, I know he was sent by God to answer my prayer request, I had just petition about a ½ hour ago, at home. How quickly God answered our request when ONE IS WALKING IN A GIFT OF EXPECTANCY. Without knowing it Richard was giving me a contribution for my "Poland Spring bottle." Richard's action definitely confirms God's answers to my petition. If seems has if Richard was in my room when I prayed to God. Certainly, he was not there when I challenged the Lord in my tiny apartment. But it is a fact, God does send out His angels to represent Him in numerous ways. Because the Bible say, God comes to us has the "Angel of the Lord." In other words, that is why it is good to be able to discern when God is answering our prayers, and do not look at a person's outer appearance. I know he was an angel sent by God to bless my life. This is what you call an "ANGELIC ACTIVITY" GOD ACTITVATE HIS ANGELS AND RELEASE THEM DOWN TO BLESS HIS CHILDREN IN TIME OF THEIR NEED. Hallelujah! Hallelujah! Hallelujah! GLORY! GLORY! GLORY! It was such a blessing to me, I could scarcely contain myself, and I kept saying "thank you King Jesus" "Thank you, King Jesus." "He is Lord." "He is Lord" Of course, I realized it was God's divine doing but never in a trillion years, did I think He would answer my supplication and, "Set me up like this." I know God has given angels different assignment one of which is to worship Him corporately as well as to fulfill His will. Hebrews 1 states, "Are they not all ministering spirit sent out to render service for the sake of those who will inherit salvation (14). "In short, what if I had not listened to God's" voice when He spoke to me, and said, "Go in the other direction." I would have missed meeting Richard and giving him, his blessing. If I did not listen to God's voice and go out to feed those in need. I would have missed God's well thought out plan, purpose, and blessing for me today.

CHAPTER 5

Fidel's Desire
9/4/15
May 12/14 3:13p.m.

It was late on Saturday night, in May when I finally arrived downtown Newark, to distribute food to the needy. The streets were terribly busy, traffic was heavy, and there were many pedestrians crossing the street. Many buses and cars were traveling back and forth. Although I had planned on being there earlier in the day, there were many circumstances that led up to why I was so terribly late. I usually try to be consistent with the time because the recipients are usually

> Amos 3:3
>
> Can two walks together, except they are agreed?

waiting. One of the major issues, why I was late, is because it was the eve of Mother's Day weekend. The saints at GLC were busy preparing a special dinner for Mother's Day at church. Moreover, I was helping in the kitchen, and assisting with a task such as grocery shopping, which helped the time to quickly slip away. Another chore was the decoration; while I was just an assistant, it took more time than we anticipated coordinating the flowers for our fabulous Mother's Day dinner.

In the end, I must say, I did enjoy fellowshipping with the saint's because we worked together for a worthy cause. It also benefited my purpose as well, since the saints happily assist me in the preparation, and packing of food, that was going to be distributed to the needy. My desire to still go even thought it was so late was confirmed by one of my sisters in Christ. Who said she would come with me on the trip downtown. However, there was no parking available when we arrived.) Yet, we were determined that we would not go back home with the meals. Furthermore, the Bible states, we must be on one accord to achieve God's work. Therefore, we got the victory. As written by the prophet Amos, "Can two walk together, except they are agreed? (3 :3) In addition, my friend did not want me to struggle by myself; with the food, so we parked as close as possible to Newark, Penn Station. Although it was a hard decision for us to separate, my friend decided she would stay in the Jeep. While I took up the challenge to carry everything. I figure it would be a piece of cake, for me to walk the few minutes, but it was still a hard task. As I walked away from the SUV, I began to "Pray and asked the Lord to give me strength to accomplish my assignment and send me help." With excitement and relief, I finally approach the bus terminal and began to feed one of the recipients, who were asleep on the sidewalk. It always breaks my heart to see human beings reduce to such conditions that they are without food and homes to live in. This site confirmed that we had made the right decision to persevere downtown. It was difficult for me to pour out the drink and hold the bags at the same time. I still need help right away. And it was then, a tall White gentleman came, rushing up to me from out of nowhere, and asked me for some money, and food. He said, "He had to catch a train to New York City." I did not have my handbag with me, and I told him so. In return, "I asked him if he could help me to hand out the drinks," And he happily said sure. After which I handed him a meal, and he was grateful to received it. I too was grateful for his help. I realized that this was the Devine hands of God, which had just heard my prayer, and send me help from one of His *"ANGEL IN DISGUISE."* Like lightening as quickly as he came, he left.

Then I cross over to Market Street to finish my mission. There were so many people online that night, at first, they were coming out slowly, and then I said "wow." It was as if I was feeding a multitude of people, just as "JESUS" did in the New Testament. When after His disciples followed Him, for 3 days He fed them bread and fish. I thought there was plenty of food for everyone, but I ran out of food. This always happens no matter how much food, I take with me, there never seen to be sufficient food for everyone. The population of the poor and needy is growing larger each time, I go downtown, Newark.

It was shortly after that, I began witnessing to a man named Peter, and Fidel came to join the conversation. He was of Spanish origin, in his mid-fifties, a majority of the needy population are Hispanic men. Fidel was eager to speak with me, about the word of God; and he was seeking encouragement. Although, he had eaten the meal provided earlier, Fidel had a spiritual hunger for the word of God. He told me his story, of how he once served the Lord, and because of the cares of this world, his relationship with God became estrange.

He said, "He was presently working on restoring his broken connection relationship with God."

However, "Today Fidel affirmed that he knows God was with him, despite the fact he was homeless."

"He mentioned that he once had a good job, and rented an apartment, however, he began to drink alcohol, and got involved with a woman."

"He explains how she later became a Christian while living with him." "Nevertheless, he did not intend to repent and change his lifestyle and she put him out."

"He realized that after he stopped serving God, all of the things he values the most were taken from him.

He said,

"God had to strip him of all his possessions for him to acknowledge God again."

Fidel says, "Although he lives in the streets, he has no regrets, if his intimate relationship with God is reinstate again."

Fidel states, "He is at peace with God, and his desire is to live for God."

Although Fidel seems to know God, I could see that he needs to spend more time seeking God, study God's word, and develop a better relationship with Him. I took the time to minister to his needs and encourage him in the Lord. As well as entreat him to come to the house of the Lord as I listen to his story. I promised Fidel, I would return. He assures me that he uses the time, he as to minister to those lost souls around him. However, he does make it clear that he too needs encouragement at times.

I Thank God, that through His perseverance my sister in Christ and I could be a blessing to those who were in need. Although our situation seemed defeated God gave us the victory, by giving us wisdom and courage to overcome the obstacles that were in our way. This night, I realized that through God's challenges came satisfaction and increase of faith in Him. As the word of God reminded us, He gives His angels charge over us to keep us in all our ways. "For he gives his angels charge over thee, to keep thee in all your ways" (Psalms 91 :11).

CHAPTER 6

Why Kathy Was Such an Inspirational Angel Sent from God to Me.
February 21/09 2:30 a.m.

While I was working at a computer two weeks ago, at the Essex County College computer lab. Suddenly a tall slender woman dress in blue jeans and a dingy gray overcoat cross my path. The anointing of God was ushered in with compassion and I felt a heavy burden on my feet. There was a heaviness laid on me in the spiritual realm for her. Realizing God was trying to get my attention; even though I did not know this woman. Nevertheless, whoever she was, she was extremely important to God. Jokingly, I said to the Lord, "You did not have to break my feet." She sat down next to me and I looked over at her and said, "Hello." I noticed she was looking at the Sunday Star-Ledger newspaper relentlessly at pictures of laptops. I said to her, "Are you looking to buy a laptop" She answered, "Yes." I was eager (on fire) to share my testimony with her about how God had blessed me with a new laptop. After waiting on Him for 4 years. I always make it a priority, to share my testimonies of God's goodness towards me with my classmates, as well as witness to them. God always seems to give me the opportunity to do so and it is a pleasure. As simple as it seems God knows all things best even if it takes forever to achieve it. As I reflected on how God had tested me before I got my laptop.

Deuteronomy 6 verse

The Greatest Commandment

[4]"Hear, O Israel: The LORD our God, the LORD *is* one! [5]You shall love the LORD your God with all your heart, with all your soul, and with all your strength.

[6] "And these words which I command you today shall be in your heart.

A months earlier, I had gone to STAPLES to purchase a lab-top on black Friday, however, I did not get one at the low price that was advertised I refuse to be online at 2 am in the wee hours of the morning, which was my special prayer time with the Lord. After all that God has done for me, I could not put purchasing a computer before Him. He is first in my life. As the Bible instruct us, we should love God with all our heart, soul, and mind. (Deuteronomy 6). One of my cousins had told me; it was the only way to get the sale price. Instead, I stayed home prayed, worshiped, and ran 8 miles, up South Orange avenue hill smiling, being grateful to the Lord for life and the ability to run at my age. In addition, I did not get there until later, however I did expect one to be on the shelve for me. But the laptops that were on sale were sold out. I was disappointed, but my faith in God is not limited. I had a little talk with God and mentioned that I did not give up on him. I assured Him that I knew He would provide for me. He led me, outside the store and to the parking lot and gave me a little job to do. I was face towards the eastbound direction to pray as the cars drove by on route 22. As well as the westbound section. It was very cold, but I swallowed my disappointment, breathe in and out, release it and prayed. A couple of months later, the laptops were on sale again at the same Staples on route 22. I decided that this opportunity would not pass me, although the price was well above my budget. My total confidence was in God. Nonetheless, when I got their God gave me a price break of half price for my laptop. I introduced myself to her. She seemed very shy and did not give me her name. Therefore, I did not pry. I began to tell her about my new laptop and her eyes lit up. However, I noticed there was something awfully familiar about her an odor, but I could not pick it up in my spirit, it was something I knew but it seemed out of place. I tried hard to identify the matter but failed and God did not tell me what it was either. God would ultimately reveal it to me soon. Subsequently, I told her to come and see it because I had it with me. Immediately she jumped up and followed me with interest and amazement! I told her it cost $800.00, but God blessed me to pay only $430.00. And later there was a rebate of $30.00 taken off. Once she saw the laptop, she seemed very enthralled in purchasing one as well. However, the more I spoke with her; I realized she would not be able to afford it. I felt really bad. Deep down in my heart I wish I could get her one, but I was not working. I told her I purchase it from "STAPLES", and she said, "She would get one." However, there was something "ELSE," God was telling me about her, that she needs a friend and I should be her friend and speak with her whenever possible. God always wants His children to consider others has He told His disciples in Matthew 5 which says, "Blessed are the poor in spirit: for theirs is the kingdom of heaven" (3). The poor in spirit are at times those who are despised in this world, look down on by many, but they are usually humble people.

Another thing I noticed as I leave for class that evening was a shopping cart in the corner filled with luggage, and it appears to belong to her. It was then it all finally came to me; although she has great ambitions, she was homeless, and still trying to achieve a college education. This was definitely something new for me, and I developed a passion to help her and find out even more about her.

I spend numerous times speaking to the Lord about her.

I wanted to know how I could help her. I took her case to the Lord like the woman in the Bible, who weary the unjust judge, because he refuses to give, her possession back. Eventually after many prayer petitions to the Lord, he answered my request. Luke 18 states, "And he spoke a parable unto them to this end, that men ought always to pray, and not to faint.

Saying, there was in a city a judge, which feared not God, neither regarded man: And there was a widow in that city; and she came unto him, saying, avenge me of mine adversary. And he would not for a while: but afterward, he said within himself, though I fear not God, nor regard man.

Yet because this widow troubled me, I will avenge her lest by her continual coming she weary me. And the Lord said, hear what the unjust judge said. And shall not God avenge his own elect, which cries day and night unto him, though he bears long with them? This parable tells what continuous prayer can accomplish, when one ceases to stop seeking God for the answer (Luke 18 1-7).

I found out that, her name was Kathy and that she was, in fact, homeless. Yet, she was making the effort to attend Essex County College to get an education. I found out this valuable information that I so desire to learn after talking to her on several occasions. It was not an easy task because Kathy was such a private person, she did not seem to trust many people; or want to let anyone into her private life. Moreover, each time Kathy and I spoke God laid a heavy burden on my heart to pray continually for Kathy, which I could not explain." It was a prayer for deliverance." Nevertheless, Kathy was so different from the others I met at Newark, Penn Station. She refused to take donations or handouts. Each time I offer her my assistance she says, "No". I had often seen Kathy in the library studying with several suitcases surrounding her. She had those suitcases because of her circumstances. I thought to myself, it must be difficult for her to struggle to school each day with all her possessions; and how hard it must be for her to focus in class, especially, since students like to stare at her. Personally, I could not understand how she manage to concentrate, on her studies but one thing I know for sure God was in the midst of her. As the psalmist sons of Korah wrote "God is in the midst of her; she shall not be moved: God shall help her, and that right early" (psalm 46). I had so much respect and compassion for Kathy, which kept me in constant prayer for her. I prayed earnestly for the Lord to bless and deliver her from her current situation. I wanted so much for her circumstances to change just to know that she graduated and succeed in life was enough for me. As a freshman, I thought if the God of Israel that I serve could do it for Kathy; He certainly could do it for me as well. As He kept the children of Israel in the wilderness for 40 years in the same clothes, and shoe and fed them manor. Being a freshman in college I was definitely in need of inspiration and Kathy was it.

She was "**An Inspirational Angel** sent from God to me."

Moreover, I "wonder if she knew it as well.""

My concern for Kathy ultimately led me to pray and questioned the Lord about, "Where she lives."

"How does she get to school?"

"How can I help her?"

"And why is it she doesn't want to accept my help?"

"What was the real purpose of us meeting each other?"

"I explained to the Lord with deep empathy, and passion that I felt helpless not being able to assist her with anything."

Eventually, one cold Saturday evening I went downtown Newark Penn Station, very enthusiastic, to leave the cares of the world behind because sometimes life gets so hectic. I just got the desire to break away; because I knew freedom was just around the corner. I had no thoughts of the homework, and exams, I left behind. It was time for me to engage my whole heart in ministry. After I fed the needy, the spirit of the Lord came upon me. He led me inside Newark Penn Station, with some women clothes to hand out. Inside Penn Station was poor lighting; also, very crowded. I was not certain who the Lord was leading me to that day, but I follow His leading. The spirit of the Lord eventually led me over to this woman with many bags on her lap and a cart filled with bags around her. She had her head bent exceptionally low and seems to be sleeping. She was sitting in the midst of many other homeless people and with a brave heart, I tapped her on her shoulder, not knowing what to expect (all I knew was that God said to do it and I did). And went she looked up it was Kathy. That day as Kathy looked up at me, I saw an illuminating bright light shining back at me.

I was shocked and marveled at the same time! I did not realize she lived downtown. I could not contain myself, "Kathy?"" I said, "With a great surprise, my mouth opens wide, and my eyes staring in disbelief." In all my years of going downtown, I would not have visualized she lived downtown! What an awesome God I serve! I had never seen her before. Truly, God is a revealer of secret. I felt like I was in heaven. I was filled with excitement; how could this be! How could God have hidden this from me for such alone time? I thought how God is a wonder and how much I loved Him for His mighty works and great acts! As the Holy Bible says in Daniel 11:32, "Those that love the Lord shall do exploit." (32). Romans 8:28 says, "And we know that all things work together for good to them that love God, to them who are the called according to his purpose." Finally, I came back down to earth and asked her if she needed anything, and she said "No!" WITH A SMILE! By the look on her face, she was also stunned to see me as well. Then she said an amazing thing to me.

She said, "You are the light," that was what she had called me one day in college when I met her in the hallway!

I thank God, she remembered me. I hugged her, and she seemed a bit embarrassed.

"She wanted to know what I was doing downtown, and I told her."

In addition, I asked her, "Why was she here?"

In return, "Kathy explained she has been without a home for a while."

"I complimented her on the good job she has been doing in school."

"And how much she had inspired my life, but she quiet me down and said, she did not want the others to know she was in college."

"I told her that Jesus loves her, and I do too." "She smiled".

"I further, tried to persuade her to encourage the others, and explained to her that if they knew she was in school, they would be motivated by her life, and eventually follow her example."

Yet, she said "No!"

"Not now"

"Later when she was finished with college, own her house, and business she would return."

Kathy exceedingly enthused me to see that her circumstances did not stop her from getting an education, by positive thinking and keeping the faith. This meeting really developed our friendship, I came to realize that all God wanted me to do at the time was just be Kathy's friend, appreciate, respect, love, and pray for her. As the Bible says show yourself friendly. Proverbs 18 states: "A man that hath friends must shew himself friendly: and there is a friend that sticketh closer than a brother." (Proverbs 23 :2).

I witness to her about the love of God. Kathy was certainly different from most of the other people, who I met because they spoke openly about their situation, but she was a reserve person. Although, most of Kathy's life was a mystery to me. I thank God for what He had revealed to me about her; and for giving me the great honor and privilege of meeting an **Inspirational Angel** like her. The smell that was so once familiar to me but seen out of place at school fell in place that day it was the smell of the *needy*. This smell usually ushers in the anointing and compassion of God in my heart to help the homeless. THINKING OF THIS MAKE SENCE but now that Kathy was downtown with the others, in the field that I love so well it all make perfect sense. I know it so well, but God certainly disguise this one. The good news about this situation is that during the summer, Kathy graduated from the Essex County College! Yes, Kathy was, "**God's Angel In Disguise.**"

My First Thanksgiving Dinner for the Less Fortunate
11/24/2000

A Homelessness affects all nationalities, and it reminds me of the Civil Right Movement which was led by Dr. Martin Luther King, which occurred during the 50s and late 60s. Dr. King fought for the rights of his people as well as for all other nationalities. He wanted Civil Rights and justice for his 4 black children, who were growing up in a white America who did not have the same opportunity as other white children. He marched for the right to integrated schools, restaurants, the right to vote, and the list goes on; black were not allowed to eat in the same restaurants as whites. They were even denied the privilege to attend the same schools, drink from the same water fountain, live in the same community and were deprived of a proper college education. Blacks were refused proper jobs although they were qualified. Why are we still facing many of these issues? Dr. Martin Luther King fought so hard for Civil Rights. Why is homelessness so evident in our society? Why is it important to feed the poor? They are human who deserve the same compassion, affection, and nurturing like anyone else. Although, I had never had the experience of preparing a large Thanksgiving dinner such as this one, I was about to take on. I was excited about the opportunity to do it. The only thing I really had going for me was that I usually helped my Grandmother, Pearline on Thanksgiving Day to prepare our family dinner. While I was not born in the United States, my family had fully adopted the American culture. Thanksgiving was one of my favorite holidays, because it was so festive. A vast number of dishes were prepared, and it was always a pleasure to assist my grandmother Pearline with the preparation of the turkey, not knowing that one day I too would face this task.

"Oh, that man would praise the LORD for his goodness, and for his wonderful works to the children of men! Let them exalt him also in the congregation of the people and praise him in the assembly of the elders. He blesseth them also so that they are multiplied greatly; and suffereth" (psalm 107; 31-38).

Above all, my greatest challenge was that I was not certain how many people I would feed. One just never know how many people would be at Newark Penn Station, on any given day because the population fluctuates. Therefore, I was thankful for the 2 extremely large turkey to feed the needy. Before starting the dinner, "I prayed and asked God to bless my hands and guide me in a divine way so the dinner would be successful." It is a good practice to give thanks in all we do as mentioned by the psalmist David.

"Oh, that man would praise the LORD for his goodness, and for his wonderful works to the children of men! Let them exalt him also in the congregation of the people and praise him in the assembly of the elders. He blessed them also so that they are multiplied greatly; and suffereth not their cattle to decrease" (plasm107 31-38).

It was 2:00 am when I began my cooking. Overall, it was not as hard as I anticipate it would be, the only problem was staying awake. I kept myself occupied by worshipping and praying. By the time, the turkeys was finished baking I was sleepy, yet I still had to bake the pumpkin and sweet potato pies. I decide to pray again. And asked, "The Lord for a supernatural awaken which was to wake me if I fell asleep." I certainly did not want to burn the house down, and if this was God's will be manifesting through my life then He would confirm it to me. I worshiped the Lord until I was tired and then went to lie down. Eventually, I did fell asleep, and was awoken by a pleasant shake on my right shoulder, although no one was in the house with me. I knew it was the presence of the Lord. I say, "Thank you Lord, and smile with Him as I got up." The smell was awesome in the house, I ran to the oven and looked at the pies, they were beautiful, I took them out the oven to cool. It was then that I became fully aware of what the Lord had done. He had blessed me to accomplish my task and I felt great in my spirit. Psalm 107, verses 21-22 says let them give

Let them give thanks to the Lord for his unfailing love and his wonderful deeds for mankind. Let them sacrifice thanksgiving and tell of his works with songs of joy. What an awesome and generous God I serve, who hears, and answered small prayer late in the midnight hours. And if that's not enough Psalm 107 reads "Oh, that man would praise the Lord for his goodness, and for his wonderful works to the children of men."(107; 31) .I just kept worshiping the Lord and said, "Thank you, Lord, for blessing me with your supernatural presence

God was not through with me yet, there was an additional dish, I needed to cook. This was not an American meal, but a Jamaican meal. To be honest this was not one of my favorite meals to prepare, because I always mess up when I prepare it. I certainly was not up to this chore for so many people, but I decided what could possibly go wrong with God's help. This dish was called, rice and peas and boy did I make a mess of it. The rice was too soft, and I felt discouraged to the point that, "I asked myself how I could serve this to the needy." I am supposed to do and give my best always because God requires me to do so. I love the Lord with all my heart and always endeavor to please Him. When He is blessing me, He always shows off and sends me more than what I need. One year, I needed a bathrobe and a nightgown, and God answered my prayer by sending me 4 of each. When they came, I laugh so hard, and I gave one to my aunt. I could not possibly wear all of them at once. I always acknowledge that what I do for others is actually God that I AM DOING IT UNTO. They deserved better and there was no more time to make another pot. I said, "Lord in a small disappointed voice, I am not going to feed the needy, because I am too embarrassed about the rice, "How can I present this to them." "Who would want to eat it?"

I felt this gentle tug in my heart that said, "Go they will appreciate it." I hesitated still insecure about my cooking." I have never felt this way before, and it certainly did not feel good. God has given me so much boldness since, I became a Christian, and now I felt inadequate. I decided to obey the Lord and packed the meals after I had a shower, which helped me to feel a little better. Yet, I could not shake the thought about what would happen, when I hand out the meals. I thought it would be a disaster when they open their meal, and I did not want to be there. I knew in my heart that if they did not eat their meal my labor would have been in vain, and I would feel even more disappointed. I reassure myself by saying "God told me to go." And if He says go, I just have to follow because He knows what's best, and not to mention why would He sends me and make me feel ashamed. Psalm 37:19 reads, "They shall not be ashamed in the evil time: and in the day of famine they shall be satisfied.

Eventually, I jump into my little black sports car and prayed again. I kept my mind on the Lord while listening to some worshipping music. I took my usual route it was a beautiful day. Once on the journey, my confidence was back but not totally, I was still thinking about the soft rice and peas. Consequently, the streets were empty due to the holiday, and only a few people were on the road. Only a limited amount of buses was in the near vicinity of downtown Newark. I park and walk for about 2 miles handing out meals as I went down Mulberry Street, and Ferry Street until I got to Newark, Penn Station.

Eventually, I handed out all the meals and was on my way back to my car, when one of the recipients came running after me,

"He was shouting did you make the food!"
"And I thought here he goes now."
"I said yes Sir, in a faint voice."
"And he said, it was great I love it."
"What?"
"I thought to myself!"
"He actually loves my cooking?"
"I laugh back with the Lord" And said, "God bless you to the man".

Once again, God was always right. What if I had neglected to go and feed the needy, just because I thought the meal was not up to my standard. I would have missed God's messenger, His celestial angel with God's message for me. "God's Angel In Disguise, came to say God was pleased with my cooking." Angels are celestials' beings who assist mankind by bringing messages of love and personal guidance. The lesson learned that day was do not doubt God under any circumstances, God knows what is best, and His will must be accomplished. He tests, His children to see if they will be loyal and obedient to Him despite their circumstances.

CHAPTER 8

The Bread Angel
May 7/2011 10:35 p.m.

I have been unemployed, for about 12 months now. Even though I had sought diligently for employment. Yet, I have not found a job or even received a job offer. As a result, of that my lack of enthusiastic for employment had taken a toll on me. My finances as depleted and it as an effect on the ministry. Whereas, while I was working, it was easy for me to afford the supplies needed to assist the poor. After a while, I began to pray and ask the Lord to open other doors of resources for me, to meet the needs of my children. I waited on the Lord in a place of expectancy to receive what God had for me, like Elijah the Tishbite, who was of the inhabitants of Gilead. When God spoke to him and said tell King Ahab, "As the Lord God of Israel liveth, before whom I stand, there shall not be dew nor rain these years, but according to my word. And the word of the Lord came unto him, SAYING, get thee hence, and turn thee eastward, and hide thyself by the brook Cherith, that is before Jordan. And it shall be, that thou shalt drink of the brook; and I have commanded

1 king 17

[1] And Elijah the Tishbite, who was of the inhabitants of Gilead, said unto Ahab, As the Lord God of Israel liveth, before whom I stand, there shall not be dew nor rain these years, but according to my word.

[2] And the word of the Lord came unto him, saying,

[3] Get thee hence, and turn thee eastward, and hide thyself by the brook Cherith, that is before Jordan.

[4] And it shall be, that thou shalt drink of the brook; and I have commanded the ravens to feed thee there.

[5] So he went and did according unto the word of the Lord: for he went and dwelt by the brook Cherith, that is before Jordan.

[6] And the ravens brought him bread and flesh in the morning, and bread and flesh in the evening; and he drank of the brook.

the ravens to feed thee there (1 King 1-4). Elijah's obedience and courage to speak God's word to the King, in a time which brought forth famine allow him to see the manifestation of God's provision in his time of lack.

By speaking the word of God with consistent prayer, God began to provide for the ministry in unusual ways, such as allowing my Bishop and his wife to assist me financially. I was grateful for their generous blessings. I knew it was the favor of God upon my life.

Last month, I had a great idea and decide to try another approached I asked God to supply an abundance of bread to make sandwiches, because I need a break from cooking. I prayed a simple prayer by faith which when like this "Lord please bless me with bread to make sandwiches for my children." I was on cloud nine just waiting on the answer. However, I did not know that because of my wiliness to help a friend with her son's birthday party, it would eventually have led to God answering my prayer. The party was festive, and many children were accompanied by their parents. God was certainly smiling down on us. It was a lovely summer afternoon everyone was relaxed. Food was being served, music was playing, and people were getting acquainted. A friend introduces me to a woman of European descent. As I stood up and greet her, she gave me a plate of food with a smile. We had met last year at this child's birthday party. I look at her and laugh. For some reason, I recognize her has the person who served me a plate of food last year. Here she was doing it again this year. Some people may call it a coincidence, but I know it was God's will for us to meet again. We began to talk, and I sense that the hand of God was in it. He was about to release supernatural miracles in my life for the ministry. I perceive this was one of His angel's, He was about to use to deliver blessings to my house. The ultimate God, as a way of using people, I would not expect to bless me. It is only through prayer and fasting, one is able to discern, the angel of God when He arrives. The omnipresent God has a great sense of style and humor in how to bless His children. Just like how, He used the angel of God in an extraordinary way to bless Manoah, and his wife after they serve the angel, they saw the Glory of God revealed in their presence. This was the angel that God sent to foretell the message of their son, Samson. "Whiles the flames were going up from the alter, Manoah and his wife saw the Lord's angels go up towards heaven in the flames. Manoah realized then that the man had been the Lord's angel, and he and his wife throw themselves face down on the ground. They never saw the angel again. (Judges 13 v 20, 21)

I replied, "You are always serving me with a smile." In return, she asked, "How was school?" And "was I employed yet?" I could feel the presence of the Lord permeating the atmosphere.

I was pleased at how concerned she was about me. Her memory was in impeccable shape. She remembered our conversation we had shared last year. I was astonished at her memory. "I mentioned that I had not found a job yet." Nonetheless, God had turned my situation around, and answered my prayer. He used my circumstances and blessed me, to be a full-time student at Essex County College. I testify to her about the change and how it occurred to me one day. While on the job working full- time;

and going to school part- time was taking too long for me to finish the 2-year program. I simply pour out my heart in prayer to God. As I worked and told, Him how difficult it was for me working so hard, and still have such a long process to finish school. I mentioned to God that I would be happier as a full-time student. So, I can have a better job. Within a few months, I was terminated from the job, while on sick leave. I was scheduled to have a biopsy on my left breast. Even though, I had filled out a request slip for time off and got coverage for the 3 days I wanted off. Yet, there was a set-up on the job. In the same way, Joseph was mistreated by his brother and thrown in a pit to die because he was his father's Jacob favorite son. I felt like I was thrown in a pit by my co-workers, who I always prayed for when they were in trouble. Yet, when I needed them to stand up for me in court they were intimidated by their supervisors on the job. My story reminds me of Joseph in the Bible. As Joseph, said to his brothers in Egypt after they had thrown him in a pit 13 years ago, and sold him to Ishmaelite's going to Egypt. Which eventually led him to Potiphar house where Potiphar's wife pursues him relentlessly to lie with her. She failed miserably and was angry with Joseph. She told Potiphar that the Hebrew slave he brought in their home tried to rape her. But as Joseph said to his brothers, what you meant for evil, God meant it for good.

> And Joseph said unto his brethren, I am Joseph; doth my father yet live? And his brethren could not answer him; for they were troubled at his presence. And Joseph said unto his brethren, come near to me, I pray you. And they came near. And he said, I am Joseph your brother, whom ye sold into Egypt. Now therefore be not grieved, nor angry with yourselves, that ye sold me hither: for God did send me before you to preserve life. For these two years hath the famine been in the land: and yet there are five years, in the which there shall neither be earing nor harvest. And God sent me before you to preserve you a posterity in the earth, and to save your lives by a great deliverance (Genesis 45: 3-7).

JOSEPHY'S MISFORTUNE LED HIM TO THE UNEXPECTED DESTINY ALMIGHTY GOD AS FOR HIM. ALSO, MY CIRCUMSTANCES LED ME TO LOSE MY JOB AND APPARTMENT ALL AT THE SAME TIME, WHICH EVENTUALLY LAND ME IN SCHOOL FULLTIME. Not to mentioned, God helped me to excel and make the dean's list my first semester at school. In view of the fact, she seemed sincerely happy for me, after listening to my story. Then I mention to her that I also prayed and asked the Lord to send me some bread for the ministry. She said, "What bread with a sparkle in her eye."

I explain to her how deep inside, my heart I just wanted to make sandwiches instead of cook meals for the needy, because it would be simpler for me to handle since I was in school. As our conversation goes on, I could still feel the presence of the Lord illuminating over the atmosphere.

"What bread?" "She replied again." "Did you say you needed bread?"

"I responded "yes," "yes,"

"I need Bread to make the sandwich for my children!" She said,

"My neighbor works at a bakery store."

"And he gives me plenty of bread."

"And I don't know what to do with it all."

"I can give you some if you like."

We were laughing at God's divine miracle and plan for us to meet again, and how He answered my prayer. Notably, she was "**God's Angel In Disguise.**" My new friend's blessing has truly been a God sent in the ministry and extended my faith in God. People, purpose, and time are enormously important in our lives as God led us to highlights and deeper debts of understanding of who He is in our lives.

After our meeting, my friend, called me numerous mornings, evenings, and nights cheerfully to remind me "She has bread for me." She always supplied me with a large quality and quantity of fresh bread, ranging from white bread, whole wheat bread, pumpernickel bread, round rolls, oval rolls, raisin bread, soft rolls for hot dogs, hoagie rolls just to name a few. Good God, I was living in bread heaven. So much bread surrounded me. Bread was distributed to shelters all throughout Newark. My apartment was filled with bread, I literally had no more room for it. My freezer was full, the fridge was packed, on top of the fridge had big garbage bags of bread. My living room had bags filled with bread too. Due to the huge quantity off supply, I dropped of bread to friends, and neighbors. Although God was using her to provide bread for me, she too had some personal issues. We often met at Dunkin Donut where I retrieve the bread. Our meetings usually end with prayer after we talked. Intercessory prayer and advise with counseling in God's word wrought deliverance in her life as well as her families.

On one occasion after our night's encounter, the *Bread Angel* called the following day, and left a message on the answering machine. It said, "I have lots of bread for you, but I know you are in school and very busy." I am not sure if I can deliver it to you. However, I will try." Because it was late that evening when I got home from school and heard the message. I said Lord; "I wish she could have e-mailed or call my cellular phone. I could have pick up the bread before coming home". Being extremely tired I could not go back on the road. I know from pass experience God was in control. If I only pray and put the situation in His divine hands, He will hear and deliver me. I fell on my knees and began to pray, "Lord I been flexible, willing, and available to go and get the bread before the school semester start. Now it is impossible for me, and I need urgent help." But I know it is not impossible for you to get the bread here to me. "If it's your will for me to continue this mission, and if you are truly using me as a channel of blessing, from now on can you, please send the bread to my house thank you." I prayed and had confidence in God; I did not call my friend. I knew God would see me through, and I was at peace with the situation. I just went back and finished my assignment. Early the next morning, immediately after I finish praying the phone rang, I decided to let the answering machine pick it up. I was too focus on getting ready for my morning run and did not want to be distracted. When I HEARD A BEAUTIFUL

VOICE, IT WAS THE BREAD ANGEL, LEAVING A MESSAGE "Marie," she said, I just found out that one of the houses I owned is two streets up from where you live." Is it ok for me to drop the bread off this morning?" "I shouted at the top of my lungs, thank you, Jesus." I express my gratitude to the Lord, by rejoicing with gladness, as I ran to answer the phone.

The following day, while on the computer seeking employment the phone rang. Again, I decided to let the answering machine pick up because I did not want to be distracted from what I was doing. However, it was the *blessed Bread Angel* calling me again with more bread. As I sat there amazed, listening I said, "jokingly aloud Lord what are You sending more bread again?"

"I did not get a chance to accomplish my task of making the first batch of sandwiches with the first set of bread she brought me." Yet I said, "Lord, it was just yesterday she brought me bread." Nevertheless, I was grateful and happy to hear her voice as well as to receive more bread. In fact, I was just telling the Lord while seeking employment on the computer, that I would go downtown tomorrow and feed the needy. He answered, "Yes", I take it that this call was to encourage, confirm, and to move me forward as plan and not to procrastinate. I suppose it was God's way of saying make the effort and do not change your mind about the mission. God knows when I am too relaxed on His job and knows how to give me a nice Holy Ghost push.

I ran to the phone and answer it, I thank her again for the bread she had given me yesterday. *The Bread Angel,* asked me what I was doing? "And I told her seeking employment on the internet." She asked, "Do you need the newspaper? And "I said sure." How did you know?" I could feel the anointing of "God all over my body." God certainly, has His *Bread Angel* on the job again. She was **God's Angel In Disguise** no doubt. Job 38:7 states, "While the morning stars came together and all the angels shouted for joy" While we are on this earth living God angels are always happy to support and assist us in our daily needs with joy. Thank you, Lord, for your abundance of angels that are sent out daily to help and rescue us from Satan clutches. It was like a dream come through because all day I was trying to figure out, how I was going to get my hands on a newspaper. I did not have any money to purchase one, has cheap as they were. I had just mentioned it to the Lord as well. When I told her my petition to the Lord, she said,

"What a blessing"

"Isn't God good?"

"I laugh."

And said, "Yes."

"He is good all the time."

I know the God I serve is the best listener in the universe. He cares about my wellbeing and those in need. Just try Him and you will see!

The Bread Angel was distributing bread very often to my house, and in return, I was distributing it through-out my community. This season of my ministry was so much fun. As I prayed and speak the word of God and send the angel of the Lord ahead of me on my trips it was successful. I laugh a lot at the results. My gift was definitely bursting out of me. I was happy helping others, and happiness was overflowing inside of me. I had a good time smiling with the Lord, as I reached each destination. Greeting the people with the joy of the Lord, and bread. Even so, there was such an abundance of bread that I ran out of people and, places to distribute it to. When God is blessing there seen to be no limit, He just keeps pouring it out like rain. All I had to do was receive God's blessings and rejoiced.

As the Bible says, "His eyes are upon the righteous and his ears are open to their cries." God hears His children, "when they cry for help," "and why they cry." Furthermore, I lived in Florida for about six months and during that time God gave me a burning desire to continue assisting the needy, in many communities. However, it was not as easy as being in Newark, New Jersey. I had to get to know the city called Kissimmee, which is in Osceola County. It was through seeking out food pantries that give out food to the needy, why I came across this fabulous warehouse that provides fresh fruits, vegetables, and bread of all sorts, and many other kinds of food for the poor. I met so many people there including the person who was in charge who gave me the opportunity of taking all the bread that were leftover, to distribute to my neighbors, as well as all over Osceola County. I place breads in mailboxes, leave them at the door, give them to whoever who open the door, seniors, children, and adults. It was while distributing the bread I met a lady, who was outside her home watering her garden which consists of oranges. I gave her bread and she gave me some huge navel oranges. They were so beautiful, and I wonder what to do with them all. She also gave me an expensive leather brown alligator handbag. I was ecstatic; we talk for a while and then she called her husband and introduce him to me. They were from the Islands; I love them so much I could see Christ in them. The kindness and love they display to me; I did not want to leave their company.

God gave me an idea to sell the oranges throughout an upper-class neighborhood, to pay my rent. I went door to door praying in my heart and rang the doorbells. I was received very well, and of course, some said no thank you. In fact, one home stood out in my memory to this day. I knew this house would purchase the remaining oranges as I approached it. I COULD FEEL IT IN MY SPIRIT HAS I rang the doorbell with confidence in God. As I wait, "I said thank you, Jesus." A teenage boy of Indian origin answers the door. I told him I was selling oranges to pay my rent and he said he was home alone; his mom was at work. I asked him if he could please call her and tell her I am at the door selling oranges and to let her know it was to pay my rent. I waited at the door and prayed again to God. Before he returns, I could feel the anointing of God all over me, and knew it was well. He came back and said, "His mother told him to take money from his piggy bank and pay me $30.00." He bought all my oranges. Of course, I was elated, stun, and hugged him." I thank God for who He knew that I did not know and also for His angels at work. Who would have known, a lady who I do not know and her son who had a heart of compassion towards me. This had to be God! And it felt good. To this day I wondered how this young man gave me money from his piggy bank without hesitation or fussed with his mother. I said to the Lord, "I learn a lesson about telling the truth and making an honest living with what you gave to me. My dear readers by listening to God and following His divine instructions that day; I could pay my rent, thanks to be to the Lord who had given me the victory. It is so good to work for God. He is my boss, had I not distributed the bread to the needy I realized I would not have been blessed to pay my rent. Readers have any of you experience anything like this, where the Lord showed up at the time of desperation and blessed you for being obedient. How did it feel? How did you react towards the person God used to bless you? Finally, how did your relationship with God change after that encounter.

Ultimately, on another occasion the Lord helped me to pay my rent by blessing me to work for Disney World. I acquired the job from a workforce labor agency. These odd jobs ranged from digging ditches picking up garbage in temperatures 106 degrees or hotter. We also had to put in temporary fences to keep- water out of the way. Besides these odd jobs gave me an opportunity to witness and pray with souls.

These experiences were adventurous and excited for me. I never knew where I would be sent to work on any given day. Thank God, I love to pray because one night I was called to go on a graveyard shift assignment to Disney World. Because I was desperate, I took the job. I was the only black woman working among some white men. I met them at a location, and we all travel together in the company's car. When we got to our destination, I was excited because of my task. I had so much energy physically from the Holy Ghost especially because I was always fasting and praying. We had to dig deep holes in the ground and replace concrete sidewalk areas that were broken down. Before we began our task, they showed me how to dig a hole. I had not a clue how to hold a shovel. I had never held one before; it was just the challenge I liked. It was easy at first.

As the Lord led, I began to tell them about Jesus. We had a good time working together. But because I was on a consistent prayer schedule, of intercessory prayers, which was basically my lifestyle. I would excuse myself at times to go and pray. To be honest, my prayer to the Lord was to give them strength to do the work. I was not surprise I could not do any more of that hard labor. Thank God for hearing and answering my prayer so quickly. I prayed so hard, that when I return, they would tell me it is ok they would do my work. I just did light duties, stood there, and prayed for God to give them added strength in my heart to get the work done. I knew it was the favor of the Lord. I used the opportunity and told them testimonials stories of God's goodness towards me.

One night I was sent out to work with another white man. He was genuinely nice. God must have been pleased with what I was doing, on the previous jobs because I was called back to work again. It is amazing the opportunities God gave me to minister to people. We spoke about God all the way back home. He was married with a family and having problems at home. I told him he need to surrender his life to the Lord, and he would change their house whole. I counsel him on some family problems he was having, and we prayed before we parted. He was such a humble man, especially for a person of his caliber. It was surprising to me that he was not a born-again Christian. He was a supervisor.

In conclusion, God kept blessing me with great bosses and His favor was evident. There was another supervisor I had who was more remarkable than all the others. It was so clear the day we met that he favored me among the others. He jokes with me and asked me questions as we travel to the job sight. By the time, we reached our destination, he practically did all my work for me. Once again, I was fasting. I laugh, and praise God as we worked in the hot Florida sun. With this job, we had to dig trenches, put up fences, and it was all done in knee-deep water. There were about four of us who worked with our supervisor. He respects and treated me so well. He even bought us lunch. I was appreciative to God for it because I was not making much money. What I earned was just enough to pay my rent, but I was extremely happy with God's blessings on my life no matter how small it was. I loved God and wanted to please Him with all my heart. As a pastor rightly told me in a women conference in 2018, "You have a strong love for God!" I thank God for the favor I found with Him and with man. As the scripture stated "So shalt thou find favor and good understanding in the sight of God and man". (Proverbs 3:4). These experiences only make me trust God even more, as He lives, breath, and moves in me. As Acts 17:28 states "For in him we live and move and have our being; as certain also of your own poets have said, for we are also his offspring. (17:28) *Thank God for all these angelic activities in my life.* Although, I felt like I was living in EGYPT AT THAT TIME IN MY LIFE IN FLORIDA. GOD SEND HIS **ANGEL IN DISGUISE** DOWN THERE TO TAKE CARE OF ME. Like Lot Abraham's cousin in the Holy Bible, thank God, I escape the destruction of Sodom and Gomorrah and return back home safely.

In view of all these occurrences, God never let down His children when they trust Him. Whether they needed bread, a job, or immediate help He finances everything, because God is our resource.

CHAPTER 9

The Mysterious Book That Was Revealed and Delivered by an Angel
September 9/6/15

Sunday is usually my day of worship. God has given us 6 days to work and the seventh day, He said to rest. Exodus 20:11 says, "For in the six day the LORD made the heavens and the earth, the sea, and all that is in them, but he rested on the seventh day. Therefore, the Lord blessed the Sabbath and made it holy". However, I had asked, "The Lord if I could use the day to feed my children (the less fortunate). I asked God for this favor because, He had blessed me with a tremendous amount of bread. I needed to use it right away before it spoils. Therefore, I was up early making hot dogs for my children. In fact, I was to pick up more bread from the *"bread angel,"* at Dunkin Donut by 4:00pm. The only way I could expedite this great task was to pray and worship God, to get strength and courage to move forward. I began to give thanks to the Lord. Psalms 136 says:

> Exodus 20:11
>
> "For in the six day the LORD made the heavens and the earth, the sea, and all that is in them, but he rested on the seventh day. Therefore, the Lord blessed the Sabbath and made it holy".

"Who remembered us in our low estate: for his mercy endureth for ever: And hath redeemed us from our enemies: for his mercy endureth forever. Who giveth food to all flesh: for his mercy endureth forever. O give thanks unto the God of heaven: for his mercy endureth forever." (23-26). Then I put on my worship music and began my ministry.

In no time the hot dogs were finished, I showered, got dressed then set out for downtown Newark. Unexpectedly, when I arrived at my destination there was a confirmation of my prayer again. There was a group of people feeding my children. It took me by surprise, but I was happy, God had sent help. Needless to say, I wondered if I was too late with the food, and would they have room for more. As I got closer to the area, I stop for a brief moment and chat with a homeless man name Joe. I have been talking to him about the Lord for the past two weeks. He is originally from Panama.

I asked him how he was doing, and he said. "O.K."

"He also wanted to know how I was doing"

"And I said, "I am blessed."

"He then asked whether I went to church today."

"And if I am coming from there?"

"I told him I did not go today."

"I asked him in return if he went to church."

And "He said he kept Saturday as his Sabbath."

As we walked, we discuss some of the financial difficulties he was having. When we reached our location, I asked Joe, if he wanted to help me hand out the food and he said, "Yes."

To my disbelief, although the other group fed the needy, the line was long. In no time, all the food was gone, and some people did not get any food. Moreover, I said, "Lord I forgot that no matter how much food we bring down here there is never enough; because there are so many people in need."

Soon after, Joe and I began to discuss the Bible and then the weather. "Finally, Joe turned to me with excitement in his eyes and said do you want to read a book I have." Although I noticed that Joe had the book, sticking out of his back pocket it never dawned on me to ask him about it. Now that he has asked, I did not answer right away. "Instead I asked God softly in my heart if it was his will." Joe looked at me. I could tell from the expression on his face, he was wondering why I have not responded to his question. So, he asked the question again. Before he could finish his question. God said, "Yes." In addition, "I said yes Joe I will read your book." However, Joe put a demand on me. He said, very sternly, "You must bring it back." He then asked me for a plastic bag, placed the book in it, as if it was a great commodity. Joe was certainly overprotective of his book. And I wonder what was in it. "Rubies?"

While attending college in the spring at West Caldwell, 9 months later. A student shoved a book in my hand in the hallway and sped off like lightning in a hurry. "I said, Lord, what was that?" I tried to pursue him, but he was nowhere in sight. As I entered my classroom. I quickly scanned the room for him, but he was not there. I hope to have seen him. It was my first semester at the college. I did not know him or much people there. As I sat down in my chair and looked at the book. I was thrilled and elated at God. He definitely knew how to show up and surprise me in a glorious way. This *angelic act* reminded me of the story in the Bible, when Peter was placed in jail, after preaching the gospel of Jesus Christ. He did not worry about being imprisoned instead; he went to sleep like a baby.

According to Gateway Bible.com

> And when he knocked on the door a servant girl named Rhoda came to answer she recognized Peter's voice but because of her joy she did not open the gate she ran and announced that peter was standing in front of the gate. They said to her you are out of your mind, but she kept insisting it was so and they said it is his angel (Acts 12 13-15).

Through divine intervention, Peter was miraculous released from prison after the church had prayed for him. God sent an angel to release him from his bondage. In the New Testament church, there was a belief that believers had angels assigned to them. So, it is today that we as children of God as angels assigned to us daily.

If I did not know it, then, I know it now, that God was constantly seeking ways to bless me. By His demonstrations of how he cares, for my needs, and how special I was to Him. It occurred to me that day, no matter what God is always the same yesterday and today. As he provides for His children in the Bible days, He also provided for me. What was significant about the book, it was the book, Joe loan me 9 months ago. This gift delighted me. What a "MIRACLE." Thank God for **The Angel In Disguise**," Joe **who** He used to bless me to read the book in the first place.

Surely, God is delightful and faithful. Although I had returned the book to Joe, I enjoyed the contents and hoped to own one. Scrupulously, enough I had prayed and asked God to bless me with one. It was a book, of great interest to me, because it relates to biblical prophecies such as those found in the book of Daniel in the Bible. There were all so other prophecies included as well. They invoke my interest, which led me to a greater insight as to what was written in the Bible. It also challenges me to read the Bible more. This confirms that God hears my prayer, because I was always seeking the Lord for more revelation in His word.

In conclusion, later that day I saw the young man (*the book angel*) in one of my classes. I told him the story about the book he had given me. He was curious has to who specifically loan me the book, and where did he get it from. I told him that it was while distributing meals to the needy downtown Newark that Joe," **God's Angel In Disguise**" loaned it to me. He laughed and mentioned that he usually passes out the books downtown Newark.

<u>READERS NOTES</u>

C H A P T E R 10

God Opened an Extraordinary Restaurant Door for the Needy
November 20 /2014 5:58p.m.

Once again, I was in need of provision to feed the needy. And decided to pray to the God of heaven to ask Him for help again. Unexpectedly, a friend of mine saw my dilemma and suggested I asked a restaurant owner to help me. She insisted one could assist me in my quest to feed the less- fortunate in my community and surrounding cities.

She said, "If you only explain to them about your mission"

I looked at her, and said, "You are right!"

"God has open doors for me before when I was in need."

After leaving my friend's presence, I laughed with the Lord and said, "You certainly did it for me before."

"So here I am again praying and requesting a favor".

"It would be a delight if you would open a door through a restaurant to help me feed your children."

I said surely,

"There are a lot of restaurant in America that throw away food they don't serve."

"If they were aware of the benefits it would bring to the poor and needy in their community; I am positive they would help."

Not knowing what God's plans were for me and His children. I prayed and believe God for the manifestation. Yet, I was not sure of where He would open the door. I thought it would be in some upscale

MATTHEW 28:33-36

And he shall set the sheep on his right hand, but the goats on the left.

Then shall the King say unto them on his right hand, Come, ye blessed of my Father, inherit the kingdom prepared for you from the foundation of the world:

For I was an hungred, and ye gave me meat: I was thirsty, and ye gave me drink: I was a stranger, and ye took me in:

Naked, and ye clothed me: I was sick, and ye visited me: I was in prison, and ye came unto me.

neighborhood. So much for my thinking, "as the word of God says, "For my thoughts are not your thoughts, neither are your ways my ways, saith the LORD. For as the heavens are higher than the earth, so are my ways higher than your ways, and my thoughts than your thoughts" (Isaiah 55:8-9). How dare me to think such a thought. Little did I know, what God was up to one night? After Ruth, Esther, and myself stepped into a fast food restaurant, to get a bite to eat. We had just finish serving the less fortunate and it was cold outside. When Ruth suggested we stop for a bite, and we all agreed. We were on a long line waiting. The atmosphere in the restaurant was noisy, and the smell of fried chicken was tempting. As we waited for our orders to be taken, we talk, and laugh. As I hand out biblical tracts. Esther shouted, "look." She was showing us someone throwing a big container of food in the garbage can." "Everyone online was stunned." What happen next, I can say that God had divinely planned it? I barely glimpsed, a large tall African American woman bending over the garbage can. She resumes her posture and walk back toward the back of the restaurant. Holding a large white container in her hand.

"I heard a man behind me gasp"

Then yell,

"Did you see that?"

Suddenly there was a frenzy of buzz on the line.

"How can they throw all that food in the garbage?"

I look, at my friend and her eyes were pop open wide. She too responds, "Did you see that Marie."

I reply, "To be honest, I only glimpse it"

All I saw was the lady's back, as she walked away with the container."

"It really puzzles me."

And I ask, "All was thrown in the garbage?"

And she replied, "Yes."

I responded, "I noticed when the individual was coming out with a huge container of fried chicken"

"But I turn to give a customer a biblical track and missed it."

Ruth was silent with her hand over her mouth

Astonished she repeated the same question to me.

"Did you see that Marie?"

"How could they do that when there are so many hungry people in our community?"

I was just pondering it when an idea pop in my heart. Ruth was right there are so many needy people in our community. And we can attest to it, because we just fed so many of them, and there was not sufficient food to go around. It is a reported fact that many restaurants around the United States throw their leftover food in the garbage. They fear being sued if someone complains of food poison or getting sick. Therefore, they dread donating the food to an organization that assists the needy. According to a blog I read called, *What Does Restaurant Do with Leftover Food*? "Some restaurants refrain from donating their uneaten foods out of fear that they believe someone may get sick, but, they have nothing to fear: thanks to Bill Emerson Good Samaritan Food Donation Act of 1996 donors are protected "from civil and criminal liability should the product donated in good faith later cause harm to the recipient or intentional misconduct." June 08, 2014(blog) (M.huffpost.com).

As I was thinking, Esther interrupted my thoughts and said, "Sister Marie, you could ask them for the food they throw away." I knew what she meant; because I was thinking the same thing and I agree with her. Surprisingly, enough it was she who told me to inquire of a restaurant and asked them to help me with my mission. It looked and felt like a set up from the Almighty God.

He does work in a mysterious way. Who would have thought the answer to my prayer would have come in this manner? I need to find out who was in charge, of this restaurant. And bring it to their attention that the food they throw away can be donated in our communities to bless the needy, who are without food and home. I mentioned to Esther, that I would come back another day and asked for the manager.

In short, this occasion was not a coincidence, but it was the will of God. It behooves us as children of God to take up the opportunity when He opens a door in our life. Whether it is for ministry or personal use.

Once at home, I prayed that evening for a 2nd confirmation. I asked the Lord, "If this was truly His plan for me to advance into it." He responded, "Yes." About a week later as I promised the Lord, I went to the restaurant after church and asked for the manager. Although, the supervisor was not there the assistant manager was available. She was very polite and of great help. She promised she would reach out to her boss and get back to me. After several attempts, we finally got the assistance we asked for. She was honest and said she was not able to get in touch with her boss, but she will blessed us with meals for the needy. The evening of the pick-up, I elaborated more on who will receive the food and how much the people would appreciate it. She finally seemed to grasp the reality of the mission. She was moved with compassion and said, "I will tell my husband that we need to go downtown Newark, this Thanksgiving with our children and feed the needy." I thank God for her kindness toward the less fortunate. As **"God's Angel In Disguise,"** she was passionate and intends to involve her family in a worthy cause because she realizes they too can be a blessing. Truly, she was already doing a great job in her community, and strategically place where God could use her for His Glory. This angel was on her way to fulfilling *her angelic duties*. As Matthew 28:35 says, "For I was an hungry, and ye gave me meat: I was thirsty, and ye gave me drink: I was a stranger, and ye took me in."

ARE YOU ONE OF GOD'S ANGELS IN DISGUISE!

CHAPTER **11**

What You Sow is What You Reap "Coins?"
November 26/2014 7:00 p.m.

Several years ago, after distributing food to the needy downtown; on a hot and hazy day. I had just returned to the car with the empty cart in my hand. When I unexpectedly stumble up on a man walking in the road seeking food. He was of small statue, frail looking, and dark complexion. He asked me for something to eat, but I told him it was finished. As I introduce myself to him, I could see the desperation in his eyes. His name was Lazarus and he was homeless. My heart ached for Lazarus because he was hungry. It appears as if he had not eaten for days and had given up hope of surviving. He was just wondering in the hot sun. His body seems dehydrated. I was silent for a while! I thought to myself, how could I help him considering there was no more meals in my bags. Eventually, I went into the car and searched my handbag for any loose change. This was hopeless because I knew it was empty. I began to look around for someone who was passing by and would assist him. No one came our way, after a while, I began to pray and asked the Lord to help me. I said, "Lord how could I leave him like this he need to be helped." Shortly, after my prayer the Lord reminded me that I had some change in the change compartment in the car. "I ran into the car again, pulled the

And Jesus sat over against the treasury, and beheld how the people cast money into the treasury: and many that were rich cast in much.

42 And there came a certain poor widow, and she threw in two mites, which make a farthing.

43 And he called unto him his disciples, and saith unto them, Verily I say unto you, That this poor widow hath cast more in, than all they which have cast into the treasury:

44 For all they did cast in of their abundance; but she of her want did cast in all that she had, even all her living.

47

compartment out with delight, there were so many coins in there." I dumped all the money in his hands." He was so excited, and I was so relieved to help someone who was in dire need. "I hug him" And said, "God bless you."

A few months later, I relocated to Alabama. It was a lovely state, but it was difficult to get a job. What was special about this state was that I feel a powerful anointing in the atmosphere. I could feel Dr. Martin Luther King Jr. spirit all over the streets, although I have never met him. As I enter my hotel room, there was an unusual awesome presence of God there. I felt God's presence so real and strong. I knew He was telling me something about myself and my purpose in this world. There was such a spiritual connection there for me, it totally knocked me off my feet. So, to speak. I felt like I was thrown, back into time to when Dr. Martin Luther King was in Selma Alabama during the 1950s -1960s. Where he achieved his most renowned and greatest successes in advancing the cause of civil rights campaigns. These protests were against racial injustices for Black Americans, as well as others who were being treated, unfairly. His devotion to this cause inspires millions of American to participate in his fight for racial equality (http://www.encyclopediaoflabama).

Another thing the Lord did was gave me a vision when I reach Alabama. After my long trip of traveling by car, fasting, and praying. As I rest my head on the bed, "I saw 2 huge hills" "One right after the other" "Each one was bigger and higher than the other." "I was startled at how high they were." "I knew God was telling me that I would be passing over these hills soon." Although I was exhausted, I sat up a bit from my vision." "And thought why God was showing me these hills?" "It was a challenged I had to face" "He knew I don't like to drive over high hills." It has been a thing from my childhood days in Jamaica. I had to walk pass an open bridge area every day to get to school and hated it. It took a lot of courage for me to walk pass it. I never complain to my aunt about it who was my guardian at the time. "Then I honestly thank God for the vision and went back to sleep." I knew He was preparing me for what lies ahead and would deliver me when the time came" "I was too exhausted to ask God any questions."

Later after my nap, I realized how hot it was, and decided I wanted to go exploring and visit the beach. Wouldn't you know it, on my way to the beach, just as God had shown me in the dream suddenly, the hills just pop up, one after the other? A medium size one then a huge hill. It happened so fast, I could hardly catch my breath or asked to turn back although I was not the one driving. Thank God, I was not driving.

To say the least, unfortunately I found myself in a similar situation like Lazarus my friend, who was mentioned in the beginning of the story. Not knowing anyone in the city and without a job I was in desperate need. I relocated to another apartment. Yet long to be in the house of the Lord, I was determined to attend church. One Sunday morning, I showered and got dress. Prayed to the Lord and asked Him to lead me to His house. Then I step out in faith and begun to walk on the sidewalk. As I pondered my journey ahead a nice gray car pulled up alongside me, and the driver an African American male asked, "Do need a ride to church?" I stare into the car and saw a family. I then asked the Lord if I should take the ride. And He said, "Yes". It certainly was a hot morning in Alabama. I would had been a fool not to have accepted! Obviously, God did not want me to walk so he provide a ride for me with a lovely family, who were **God's Angels in Disguise."** "God is awesome the family in the car was on their way to church and they took me with them. I told them my story. How I was new to the community and came out by faith to get a ride to church. It is amazing how God always provides for His children with such simplicity and grace. When we reached our stop, it was a huge Baptist church. This was surprising to me. God knew I was baptized in an apostolic church. In the "NAME OF JESUS", but who knows what He had in mind for me. God is utterly amazing when I got there it was evident the Holy Ghost was there. Thank God for His **"Angels In Disguise"** He send to escort me to church. God's spirit was moving through the congregation. This was news to me, because I did not know the Baptist denomination had the spirit of God abiding with them so fluently. Something wonderful happened in my life that day God revealed Himself to me through a mother in the church. The whole congregation was worshipping God in the isles when an elderly Mother came up to me and prayed with me. She senses all that was occurring in my life, and what I was fearful of. She send Michael the ark angel home with me. I was totally amazed at the things she revealed about my life. It was God's doing. I was happy for the prayer which I did not asked for and welcome my angel Michael home with me. From that summer of 2002 I also took along Gabriel the ark angel home with me. Since, that moment I knew God was working in my life and working it out for me. I was so elated after returning from church and had a deep desire to return.

Nonetheless, I was unable to return there, but God directed me to another church. While attending the church service one evening at a Pentecostal church for the first time. An African American lady came up to me with a smile, after service. She gave me a handful of change. And said, "If you return later, I have something else for you." This was definitely **"God's Angel In Disguise,"** I took the gift and was in awe. Her actions and kind-heartedness reminded me of the story in the Bible where a poor widow woman gave all she had. Mark 12 reads:

And Jesus sat over against the treasury and beheld how the people cast money into the treasury: and many that were rich cast in much. And there came a certain poor widow, and she threw in two mites, which make a farthing. And he called unto him his disciples, and said unto them, Verily I say unto you, That this poor widow hath cast more in, than all they which have cast into the treasury: For all they did cast in of their abundance; but she of her want did cast in all that she had, even all her living (MARK 12: 41-44).

The widow mentioned in this story did not have much money, but she gave sacrificially to God without hesitation. Jesus saw their generosity and honesty and take note of it, that how we are to be as children of God and give as He commanded; and he will do the rest when we are in need. I did not know why this lady whom I met for the first time was giving me her last money in her purse, but I was appreciative for her donation. I hugged and thanked her. I told her, "Good Lord's willing I would see her later." I was anticipating in my heart what surprise God had planned for me next. He certainly knows how to blow my mind. Off course, I did not want to miss it for anything in the world. As I walked away from her presence, thanking God, for His astonished giving through her. Though grateful for the money, it also puzzled me.

"Why had I received so many coins?"

"Why not one dollar, or five dollars." This was my thoughts and question to God, as I walked out of the sanctuary, talking, and laughing with Him. Nevertheless, God did not respond to my questions. It makes you think how sometimes one would have a conversation with God, and He give you no answer. Yet, He is listening. Even though you repeated it, He does not respond, but He is God. It is a fact; He does answer in His own time. At home that evening, I express my gratitude to the Lord by worshiping. I sang, at the top of my voice in the spirit and danced in the spirit. Clapped my hands under the influenced of the anointing and ran through the apartment. I had picked some lovely flowers for God on my way home. For years I have been taking home flowers for the Lord when I go running. I love the Lord so much and I tell Him so often in one day. Saying, I love you Lord is not enough for me, I must put my words into action. It brings such a lovely feeling to my heart to pick fresh flowers for Him. I usually bow in His presence as I present them to my King. After which they are place in water on the dresser in my bedroom. I looked at them and laugh, as it dawns on me just how much the beauty of them brightens my day. How ironic it is God who create flowers and here I am giving them back to Him. What can I really give to God that He has not created even my heart He gives me? In my excitement, I throw the coins on the bed and laugh. "God is good." "God is good to me."

It was later that evening, while quietly at home meditating on God's goodness, "He reminded me of my generosity to the less fortunate man in New Jersey." While I sometimes forget the events of my life God does not. I was oblivious to what God was doing in my life. There have been times when the Holy Ghost allows me to discern what was coming in my life, and at times through dreams and visions. Yet, at other, instances He totally surprises me, and hide things from me. I know God enjoy this too. However, I must say that I am a very curious person and desire to know more about God and how He works in my life as well as others.

I now realized why it was so important for me to have helped the homeless man. Although I did not know it then, that I would need a helping hand, some day from someone. I certainly know it now. That is why it is as vital for us as human being to be considerate about others well-being. Who knows when they will find themselves in similar situation as those living on the streets? The Bible says," Then Peter opened his mouth, and said God is no respecter of persons" (Acts 10:34). I must say it felt good to have someone, whom I did not know or told my problems blessed my life. God is good! It is obvious to me when He is using an individual to fulfill His desire towards me. I thank God for sending His angel to assist me in a city where I knew no one except Him. Apostle Paul had and experience in the Bible where he too was in a city and knew no one, but God was his help. Acts 18:10 states one night the Lord spoke to Paul in a vision: Do not be afraid; keep on speaking, do not be silent. "For I am with you, and no one is going to attack and harm you, because I have many people in this city" (Acts). In short, I learn what you sow is what you reap has the bible says. Upon the confession of her word, the faithful sister came back that night to service and gave me $ 20.00. In return, by faith, I sowed it into the ministry because they were having their pastor's appreciation service. It seems just the right thing to do, knowing God would continue to take care of me while in Alabama. God's faithful angel was a tremendous giver and a blessing to my life. I can see that she was one who enjoys her duties in the church ministry and listen to God when He speaks to her. Pertaining to those in need and how much to give, she certainly has an eye of discernment. Given these points, I can only imagine when other visitors come to that house of God and received their blessings, they return to thank the Lord. As the 1 leper, out of the 10 whom Jesus healed, who returns and told Him thanks. According to Luke 17

And it came to pass, as he went to Jerusalem, that he passed through the midst of Samaria and Galilee. And as he entered into a certain village, there met him ten men that were lepers, which stood afar off. And they lifted up their voices, and said, Jesus, Master, have mercy on us. And when he saw them, he said unto them, go shew yourselves unto the priests. And it came to pass, that, as they went, they were cleansed. And one of them, when he saw that he was healed, turned back, and with a loud voice glorified God, and fell down on his face at his feet, giving him thanks: and he was a Samaritan.

CHAPTER 12

The Man Who Once Owned A Popular Radio Show
December 20, 2014 4:00p.m.

It was late one night, after I had just fed the needy at Newark Penn Station, and was wrapping up when I bumped into a verbose man. He was in his mid-50s. I look up from my bags and said, excused me, but he seemed delighted to see me. He was dressed in black business attire and carried a black leather briefcase. He was eager to talk with me. Yet, honestly, I was focusing on telling the others Good-bye. He kept right on following me talking. I just did not get it at first. He was relentless with his pursue to speak with me. I did not respond to his simple comments as well as, when I was finish tending to the others; he finally got my attention, and I asked him his name. He replied, "Bob." "Then I asked him where he was going?" "And if he was waiting for the train?" And he said,

> Mark 12
>
> And the second is like, namely this, Thou shalt love thy neighbour as thyself. There is none other commandment greater than these.
>
> 32 And the scribe said unto him, Well, Master, thou hast said the truth: for there is one God; and there is none other but he:

"No." He was inquiring if I ever heard of a particular radio show on the AM station, and I said no. I really did not know who he was or why he was asking me so many questions. He replied, "You never heard of it?" Again, "I said no?" "I asked him why he was so interested in whether I had heard of that radio station," He said, "I used to own it." "I said what?" He said, "Yes" I owned it for many years", "FINALLY HE CAUGHT MY INTEREST" "I asked what happened." He said, "He lost it along with his home and was currently homeless." Although it cross my mind that he too may be homeless, I did not enquire of the Lord his status. Also, did not want to jump to any conclusions. I looked at him in dis believe was he for real. I wonder in my thoughts. He continued to say, Penn Station has been his home for a while. I was still trying to comprehend what he told me. It took me by surprise he certainly did not look like he was homeless or in need. I supposed his demeanor throw me off guard, and off course, this was my first time seeing him. Not to say, that all the poor and needy are dress in rags and push a shopping cart or carry their clothes in black garbage bags or in a suitcase. Thank God, some have access to public facilities which allow them to take care of their daily hygiene and certainly he was one of them, who maintain it. As I listen to him, spoke of his misfortune, it opens up my understanding as to how people can become homeless base on different circumstances of life. This man was so rich and affluent in his community and now living at Penn. Station. It occurred to me that homelessness could happen to anyone, even to the best of us. And, the loss of financial revenue plays a major part in why so many people, of diverse ethnic group, are without homes. Yet, it is our responsibility has a society not to look down on such a person, but to help to restore such a person, who have fallen by the way. One way of helping it is by assisting them with a decent place to live as well as provide jobs for them. Helping the less privileged as well as those struggling to get back on their feet will better humanity. Suddenly, after hearing his story, I found myself wishing I could be of some assistant to this man, who could have been my father. It truly does not matter one's race, creed, or ethnic background, all that matters is that someone is in need. As the Bible says we should love our neighbor as we love ourselves, and if we absolutely love our self would we want to give them the best. We would not want to look dirty or smelly?

According to Mark 12,

"And the second is like, namely this, thou shalt love thy neighbor as thyself. There is none other commandments greater than these.

And the scribe said unto him, well, Master, thou hast said the truth: for there is one God; and there is none other" (Mark 12: 31-32).

Here God commandment instruct us to love our neighbor. Who then is our neighbor it only those who live next door to us? No, our neighbor is anyone in need and if we value our life then as God children, we too should value others. And if we fall into this condition would not, we want someone to help to restore us back to humanity. Bob's story reminds me somewhat of Job in the Old Testament although Job was a man of integrity and did nothing wrong, God tested him. He eventually lost all his possession, including his 10 children, and was stricken with boils on his skin, yet he held on to his faith in God. Even though by no means, this gentleman was physically sick, he had lost his wealth just like Job and was homeless. Nonetheless, it was apparent that although this gentleman was living on the streets, he was still trying to maintain his integrity. If he did not reveal his identity, who would know he was homeless except the spirit of the Lord reveals it. He was determined to get his life back on track, I had so much empathy for Mr. Bob, and it was a privilege and honored, that he shared his life story with me.

I can say that homelessness is absolutely faceless base on the majority of people, who I have met from all social classes from rich, poor, educated, non-educated, whites, blacks and Hispanic and the list goes on. It can occur to anyone for example me. I am no exemption, often I asked the Lord, "why not me." I too am struggling, as a college graduate I have not been able to attain a decent job since 2010. Nevertheless, it is the grace of God that is keeping a roof over my head. And kept me in good health, a sound mind, food on my table, and shoes on my feet and a car to drive. God always supplies my basic needs and I am grateful to him. After meeting with Mr. Bob that night, I never saw him again at Penn Station although I sought for him. I wonder up to this day was he one of **GOD'S ANGELS IN DISGUISE,** God sends to test me in the field. One never knows who God would place in their path. As I mention earlier in the story, I was so preoccupied with the needy and focusing on my getting home that I particularly ignore this gentleman but thank God for his patience with me to hear him out. According to Mark 16, "And entering the tomb, they saw a young man sitting on the right side, dressed in white robe, and they were alarmed. And he said to them, "Do not be alarmed. You seek Jesus of Nazareth, who you crucified HE HAS RISEN HE IS NOT HERE. (Mark 16: 5,6). Hence, as one can see even Jesus Himself had His own angels to help Him while he was on earth. In order, for Jesus to come out of the tomb where He was placed for 3 days, an angel had to assist him by rolling away the stone. This gentleman came as **"God's Angel In Disguise,"** to roll away the stone of blindness from my eyes.

IT'S GOOD TO BE FREE HAS A BIRD

SPECIAL THANKS TO CARRETTA _POWELL_ MY COUSIN WHO IS MY DIGITAL FOLDER PHOTOS ORGANIZER. THANKS FOR ALL YOUR HELP.

CHLOE IN HER BALLET CLASS
SHE WEIGHED 1 POUND 6 OUNCES WHEN SHE WAS BORN!

CHAPTER 13

The Educated Woman Who Lost Her Home
December 21/14 8:10 pm

It was a cold, and briskly day in Newark. As I push my red cart toward the bus stop, I was on my way back home tired from assisting the needy. Because it was so cold, I was in a hurry to get to my car. Despite, my efforts, to reach the needy in the wintertime to feed them it was still not enough, because they have no respite or permanent shelter over their heads. Many of them still refuse to stay in the shelters, because of the bad conditions and the treatment they receive such as theft of their valuables. They often complain that while they are asleep someone stole their belongings. As I reflected upon how the cold weather numbed my hands and feet, it dawned on me that the poor and needy were going through a worsted time than me. My heart and soul go out to them, and it causes me to wonder how God's grace and mercies truly kept them in conditions such as, below freezing temperature, snowstorms and, even blizzard at times through the whole winter. I often prayed, cried at times, and asked God to watch over them while I am not there, although I know God is omnipotent. Not that I am not aware that He is in control of their situation, and he knows all the details already, God wants us to have compassion on others. It is my heart's desire and heart's cry to God for them to have a permanent home, and be restored back to the community, and know their purpose and rightful place in this world before he returns for His children. I do acknowledge the Bible does say the poor we will have with us always. Jesus acknowledges "the poor you will always have with you, and you can help them anytime you want. But you will not always have me (Mark 14-7).

> Proverbs 12
>
> [17] He that speaketh truth sheweth forth righteousness: but a false witness deceit.
>
> [18] There is that speaketh like the piercings of a sword: but the tongue of the wise is health.
>
> [19] The lip of truth shall be established for ever: but a lying tongue is but for a moment."

It was then I ran into an elderly African American woman. She was dressed in gray, jogging pants, sneakers, and a heavy winter coat. It truly breaks my heart to tell her that the food was finish. She was more interested in having someone to listen to her problems than having food once we were introduced. As I listen to her, spoke. What was intriguing about her was her voice; she was highly intelligent. She told me that she used to be a homeowner, with a prestigious job. But she lost it all and today she is living at Newark, Penn Station. As I listen to her story, it baffled my mind; her story was so like the white gentleman mentioned in the previous chapter. The question that ran through my mind was how someone could once own so much wealth and suddenly lost it all just like that. Once again, this subject was remarkably interesting to me, and I need to learn more about it. Just like, so many I have spoken to in the past, she was so candid about her life. I felt sorry for her and realize it must have been devastated to own your house and now lives on the streets. Although this person had gone through such an ordeal, she was humble, and definitely still incredibly grateful to Almighty God. In fact, she did not blame God for her homelessness. Instead, she has a regretful heart, and testifies that it was her fault she lost her home, because of an addiction to alcohol. Which eventually led her into a different type of lifestyle that involves doing things that go against her moral standards? She notes sadly that to maintain her addiction she lost all her possessions. Nonetheless, she now put her focus and emphases on God and said she still loves God despite losing everything. It was just remarkable to learn about all this woman had suffered and yet she held no resentment towards God. This really makes me wonder what if I had possessed what she had and lost it all. I know that God is number one in my life, and earthly possessions are temporary, and spiritual inheritance is eternal. Would I still desire to serve God? After facing such an issue many people would blame God for their calamity and refused to acknowledge Him again. Although this woman lost her American dream, because of her owned addiction, she still believed in God and that He would help her to recover all. Proverbs 12 says, "He that speaketh truth sheweth forth righteousness: but a false witness deceit. There is that speaketh like the piercings of a sword: but the tongue of the wise is health. The lip of truth shall be established forever: but a lying tongue is but for a moment" (17 -19).

In conclusion, her story was so intriguing to me; it makes me forget how cold I was. It was a pleasure for her to share her story with me. If for no other reason it makes me see what can happen to me, when I achieve wealth and forget the God who help me attain it. For example, God warns Israel before they got to the promise land Canaan not to serve the Canaanite's idols or he would destroy them. This account comes as a reminder for me, that having possessions is not the answer to a prosperous life, but instead, it is true happiness from inside which flows to the outside. Anyone can achieve this kind of success by doing the things that God has place in their hearts and spirit to do. Finally, knowing who God really is; so, when He does bless me, I do not lose focus on who the blesser is! To say the least, this was **"God's**

Angel In Disguise." An angel of warning in disguise. That attaining to monetary things and going up the ladder so to speak has a cruel way off bringing one down, if they get too proud and forget those who help them along the way or worst for get God. One message that the Lord send to our congregation about 2 years ago is "Don't forget God" "When He bless you." And it is a message that I continue to pray to God to help me never to forget Him because of money, or else I do not want it. Besides my soul is more important than money.

CHAPTER **14**

The True Meaning of Christmas Revealed
December 25/14 12:30pm

Christmas Eve was one of my favorite moment with the needy. It was a tradition to hand out gifts. On this particular cold night, I had just handed out the last Christmas gift at Newark, Penn. Station. But, from experience, even though I enjoy this time of year, it was usually hard for me to encounter anyone after the gifts were all gone. It is a horrible feeling to face the needy when you have nothing to give them. In short, I was heading towards my car; when I ran into a slender African American young woman, who was homeless. She was a pretty lady with bright eyes. She came up to me expecting to get a gift, and I felt hopeless. I had nothing to give her, and I told her so. Suddenly, the Lord spoke to my heart to explain to her about the real purpose why we celebrate Christmas, and I began to minister to her about it. I explain to her about Mary the mother of Jesus, and how God chose her to be Jesus's mother. I expounded a bit further on the story and told her how the angel Gabriel told Mary she shall bring forth Jesus through Immaculate Conception.

Luke says,

> Luke 1, verses26-28
>
> 26 And in the sixth month the angel Gabriel was sent from God unto a city of Galilee, named Nazareth,
>
> 27 To a virgin espoused to a man whose name was Joseph, of the house of David; and the virgin's name was Mary.
>
> 28 And the angel came in unto her, and said, Hail, thou that art highly favoured, the Lord is with thee: blessed art thou among women.

"And in the sixth month, the angel Gabriel was sent from God unto a city of Galilee, named Nazareth to a virgin espoused to a man whose name was Joseph, of the house of David; and the virgin's name was Mary. And the angel came in unto her, and said, Hail, thou that art highly favored, the Lord is with thee: blessed art thou among women. And when she saw him, she was troubled at his saying and cast in her mind what manner of salutation this should be. And the angel said unto her, Fear not, Mary: for thou hast found favor with God. And behold, thou shalt conceive in thy womb, and bring forth a son, and shalt call his name JESUS. He shall be great and shall be called the Son of the Highest: and the Lord God shall give unto him the throne of his father David: And he shall reign over the house of Jacob forever, and of his kingdom, there shall be no end (1: 26-33).

The story brought interest to her and opened her understanding to revelation. She told me that from her youth she was told that the only reason we celebrate Christmas was for the sole purpose of giving and receiving gifts. I told her no, Jesus died for her sins and mines and to redeem us unto Himself. Her eyes began to get bigger and brighter. And she replied, "That's the reason we celebrate Christmas?" In fact, there was such a change in her countenance, and her face shined it was clear that the mystery of Christ birth has been revealed to her by the Holy Ghost. I also told her that Jesus loves her that why He died for her sins. According to King James Version of the Bible which states "And she shall bring forth a son, and thou shall call his name JESUS; for he shall save his people from their sins" (Matthew 2). As I concluded the story she shouted, I got it! "Now I know the true meaning of Christmas." Her expression changed again, and I perceived the Lord had converted her heart. I promised to bring her a Bible the next time I visit downtown. I could see that the angel of the Lord had definitely touched her heart; and before I could utter another word she ran away hastily and happy. I knew in my heart she was on her way to tell others the good news. She reminded me of the Samaritan woman, whom Jesus met at the well in Samaria. When Christ was revealed to her, she too ran into the city, "Telling everyone about Him that told her everything about her life and how He changed her, those who listen to her story receive salvation as she spread the good news." (John 4). Just as God use the angel Gabriel to foretell the message of Jesus' birth to Mary, it is so Jesus uses us sometimes as **God's Angels In Disguise** to tell others He is the God of their salvation.

CHAPTER 15

I was Like the Shunamite Woman This Christmas
December 25, 2014 12:45pm

The past few months have been a struggle for me financially. Realizing that God was my only source as brought about a significant sense of humility and dependence on Him, solely for my daily needs. Have you ever bought groceries from a supermarket and was not pleased with it and could not return it because you lost the bill? After much prayer and being frustrated by the process of throwing money in the garbage. The Lord taught me how to save money on groceries. By blessing me to shop at a splendid supermarket which allows me to return groceries if I was not satisfied with them. Although, at the time some of the items were opened. What makes this supermarket spectacular was that it did not require a receipt to return items. Or place a time limit on when one should return the things. One just had to return the remainder of the merchandise as it was convenient for them. There were no restrictions. The opportunity was given to everyone to exchange items or get one's money back. The convenience of this special supermarket helped me to use God's money wisely. Stopped me from throwing out groceries in the garbage due to lack of satisfaction. I was able to save money this way and utilize my funds as best as possible. In other words, I wanted to be a good steward of God's money. It was my

5 I am the Lord, and there is none else, there is no God beside me: I girded thee, though thou hast not known me: That they may know from the rising of the sun, and from the west, that there is none beside me. I am the Lord, and there is none else.

7 I form the light, and create darkness: I make peace, and create evil: I the Lord do all these things.

8 Drop down, ye heavens, from above, and let the skies pour down righteousness: let the earth open, and let7 righteousness spring up together; I the Lord have created it.

(Isaiah 45:5- 8).

understanding from reading scriptures that if God can trust you with a little, He can also trust one with abundance. Depending on God meant; I had to pray consistently although the requests were basic. They require me to pray. God does know how to get one's attention and through prayer, I can connect with God and pull on His resources. My prayers were specific, by faith with high expectation from God. One day it dawns on me that I was in need of, money to buy Christmas gifts. As I pondered it in my heart what must I do about my dilemma? The Lord reminded me that I had some money. It was money I had deposited down on graduation pictures. Regrettably, time did not permit me to fulfill the obligation. I was thrilled and hoped the photographer would remember me because six months had passed since we finished the transaction. In short, I was counting on his integrity to return the money. Looking back now, I know understood that everything God allows to happen in my life was for a purpose and for His "GLORY". In fact, God does have an appointed time for things to happen in my life.

He was a true Gentleman "**God's Angel In Disguise.**" When we spoke on the phone, and he generously wanted to return the money immediately. The only problem was it was not convenient for me to accept it from him myself, at the time he was available. However, God would have it that he was meeting with two of my friends the following day. He promised to give the money to them. Since I could retrieve it later after work. The remarkable thing about this situation was that had not God reminded me of this forgotten money I would not be able to purchase Christmas gifts for the needy. Christmas was just around the corner and I was definitely in a tight spot because I only worked 3 hours per day. "Who says God does not answer prayers on time?" Yes, **I CAN SAY FOR A FACT GOD IS AN ON TIME GOD**" I had decided that I would not let my current situation get the best of me and trust God. He would, "Make a way out of no way and provided for the need of the less fortunate." All these occurrences, lead me to put total trust in God because he says in Isaiah,

"He creates good and evil. I am the Lord, and there is no one else. I form the light, and create darkness: I made peace, and create evil: I the Lord do all these things" For Jacob my servant's sake, and Israel mine elect, I have even called thee by thy name: I have surnamed thee, though thou hast not known me. I am the LORD, and there is none else, there is no God beside me: I girded thee, though thou hast not known me: That they may know from the rising of the sun, and from the west, that there is none beside me. I am the LORD, and there is no one else. I form the light, and create darkness: I make peace, and create evil: I the LORD do all these things. Drop down, ye heavens, from above, and let the skies pour down righteousness: let the earth open and let them bring forth salvation, and let righteousness spring up together; I the LORD have created it. (45:1-8).

Not having a full-time job does not mean God would not provide the necessary revenue I need for His mission. After all, He is sovereign and in control of everyone life.

Finally, because I obeyed God the money was returned to me just on time to buy Christmas gift, for those in need. In some respect, I can say God as provided for me as He provided for the Shunamite Woman in the Bible. After the prophet Elisha instructed her to leave her home because the Lord had called for a famine. She traveled and stayed with the Philistine for 7 years. It was her excellent services and obedience to Elisha that brought the blessing into her life. Being a well to do woman she perceives Elisha was A HOLY MAN OF GOD. And she builds a chamber for him to stay in her house when he passes by. Note in the beginning of the chapter Elisha asked her if she wanted the King or commander to know about her kindness toward him and she replied no "I just want to dwell among my people." And he said to him, "Say now to her, 'See, you have taken all this trouble for us; what is to be done for you? Would you have a word spoken on your behalf to the king or to the commander of the army?'" She answered, "I dwell among my own people." (2 Kings 4 :13) Her obedience to God and His servant later brought her honor and recognition by the king without her knowing consent. It took God's divine plan to use Elisha to bless her life as well as the king's curiosity which, got the best of him. Upon the king asking Grahamite Elisha servant about the miracles God had wrought through him. What was every fascinating to me, was that the Lord was the one who called for the famine in the Land, and told Elisha to instruct her to leave? It is amazing how when God wants to perform a miracle in one's life, He does some radical things so one can glorify His name and appreciate Him more. After this lady had gone through her faith being tested God restore her property plus the inters from the seven years she was away.

2 Kings 8 :1 says: "Then spake Elisha unto the woman, whose son he had restored to life, saying Arise, and go thou and thine household, and sojourn whosesoever's thou canst sojourn: The Lord hath called for a famine, and it shall also come upon the land seven years" (Biblegateway).

In comparison, after reading about the Shunammite's woman faith in the Bible and how God restored her land, I know God allows me to be in certain situations, so He can test my faith. In trusting God, He is able to provide for me. Only, if I surrender totally to His, will for my life.

In a word, I will reap the abundance of benefits, He as for me. That is why prayer is important. I have to seek the Lord daily in prayer and listen for his instruction for my life, or else I will be lost. Sometimes God sends our blessing in disguise just like the angels He uses to deliver them.

CHAPTER 16

An Abundance of Pretzels
June 26, 2015 8:32 am

Sunday morning began with prayer at God's house, it is our custom to have early morning prayer, and I was excited about being there. This morning because I had a prayer request for myself, I have been going through a season of storms all related to unusual sicknesses, I had never experience. I had sought the Lord on these issues as well before because one moment I was well and the next instant I was sick again. The symptoms were even worse at times. Although there were not many saints out for morning prayer that particular morning, God used my sister's in Christ to pray and I was delivered mightily. I felt so free after the anointing of God felt on me, it when right through my very being. I worshiped and thank God. I knew my struggles were over, and no matter what I had trusted God, because "GOD IS A GOOD GOD." The scripture that was read that morning was Psalms 27, "which was our foundational scripture usually read.

Psalm 27 says:

And he shall set the sheep on his right hand, but the goats on the left.

Then shall the King say unto them on his right hand, Come, ye blessed of my Father, inherit the kingdom prepared for you from the foundation of the world:

For I was an hungred, and ye gave me meat: I was thirsty, and ye gave me drink: I was a stranger, and ye took me in:

Naked, and ye clothed me: I was sick, and ye visited me: I was in prison, and ye came unto me.

One thing have I desired of the LORD, that will I seek after; that I may dwell in the house of the LORD all the days of my life, to behold the beauty of the LORD, and to enquire in his temple. For in the time of trouble he shall hide me in his pavilion: in the secret of his tabernacle shall he hide me; he shall set me up upon a rock. And now shall mine head be lifted up above mine enemies round about me: therefore, will I offer in his tabernacle sacrifices of joy; I will sing, yea, I will sing praises unto the LORD. Hear, O LORD, when I cry with my voice: have mercy also upon me and answer me. When thou said, seek ye my face; my heart said unto thee, thy face, LORD, will I seek (27, 4 -8).

Later, that morning, I was in a rush to Sunday school, because I promised God I would be there and decided that I would not let anything stop me, from being there. The topic that I read in the Sunday school lesson had caught my attention. It was on evangelism, remarkably interesting, motivating, and I wanted to learn more about it. But something caught my eye as I drove down a narrow one-way street, at the stop sign. There was a church on my right-hand side of the street and a gentleman (guard) standing by the fence trying to stay out of the sun. It was super-hot that day. I saw two tables in clear view with a sign marked free. The tables were filled with huge pretzels like the one's vendors sell at carnivals and street events. I have often talked to God about being spontaneous on Sundays and just go has He leads me in ministry because there are fewer ministries feeding the needy on that day. Now, that the Lord was showing me an abundance of pretzels', I thought was He challenging me, to do something different out of the norm. I always love that kind of surprise and adventure. As the scripture state, they that know their God shall be strong and do exploit. Daniel the prophet who was carried off to Babylon in 605 B.C by king Nebuchadnezzar wrote, "But the people who know their God shall be strong and do exploits (11:32). This was a big moment for me, I could not resist. Yet deep down inside I wonder what God really wanted me to do with these pretzels, was I to leave them? On the other hand, should I take them along? Nevertheless, from experience with God, I knew this was a setup, but would I take the challenge. Alternatively, was I just all talk? I looked to God for help and felt confident it was His perfect will. As I approached, the table a man steps out from under the shady spot where he was staying cool from the heat, said "You could take all, and there are more inside. "ALL" I responded, I LOOK AT THE MAN, AND SAID TO MYSELF "WHERE WAS I GOING TO PUT IT?" "I AM IN A HURRY I TOLD MYSELF." I WANTED TO CRY AND LAUGH AT THE SAME TIME. IT WAS RIDICULOUSLY HOT OUTSIDE. ALTHOUGH, I HAD LEARNED TO BE GREATFULL FOR THE HEAT AND NOT COMPLAIN BECAUSE HELL WAS HOTTER. HOWEVER, I WAS SWEATING LIKE CRAZY, AS IF I JUST GOTTEN OUT OF THE SHOWER. I SUPPOSE GOD WAS JUST WAITING FOR ME TO MAKE THE FIRST MOVE.

I thought long and hard about my Sunday school lesson. "What was God really up to this morning?" I had my plans. But His will must be done. All I needed was right in front of me included bags to put the pretzels in. I introduce myself to the gentleman, his name was Ricky. Lord, I said you brought everything that was in my heart to pass as I packed them up.

I told the guard Rickey, that I would take them to the poor and needy downtown, Newark. I realized it must be a big joke to God because Rickey kept bringing out more pretzels, and I began to laugh. God was encouraging me to take them through Ricky's actions. It was definitely too many pretzels and I was having excessively too much fun. I did not bargain for such a time with the Lord this morning. I kept saying to the Lord, "I know these are not for me." Sure enough, God had a blessing there just for me as well. I had just about finished my salt at home, which I use to soak my feet after running this morning, and I needed more. I knew God would supply my need, but I did not know when. I know the real test of being a child of God is waiting on God and trusting Him to provide when one is in need and not tell anyone. He as a way of showing up when you least expect Him. Ricky gave me some salt, and I was laughing because God was too much in this place. Moses wrote in Genesis 28, that Jacob the father of the 12 tribes of Israel had a vision from God, "And he dreamed, and behold a ladder set up on the earth, and the top of it reached heaven: and behold the angels of God ascending and descending on it (28:12). Sometimes God can be in a place, and because of the way it looks, you doubt His presence until He began to reveal Himself. Ricky said, "I will be right back". He disappeared inside the church and brought out an abundance of salt. It was clear, there was no way out. I said, "Lord I know you want me to feed the needy, but I want to leave some for someone else. As I finish speaking a man came by, it was God's doing and I was relieved when he came and took some of the blessings. Yet it seems as if God did not want me to leave that spot, just yet. I was thinking about going to Sunday school, after all, I got the Sunday school message, and it was time to put it in action. God brought someone for me to witness to, the lesson was not just for me to read and leave it in the book but to put into practice. Upon reaching the church, I place the pretzels in a cool place.

It was later after church, that I decided to take the pretzels to the poor and needy, but there was one problem. Since this blessing caught me off guard, I needed a flat pair of shoes or slippers to wear. Nonetheless, I was depending on God to provide one for me, because He as to complete what He started.

God never fails! There is a sister at church God has been using for years to bless me; with shoes or slippers, in unexpected cases like these. But this time, I did not know where God would get His shoes from because I know that she had run out. Nevertheless, listening to God, I approached her and asked for a pair of slippers. She had given me about 5-6 pears already, and the last one she gave me; I told her I would return it, but she always says no keep it. I cannot say this time if I was expecting a slipper or not because this knowledge of her possibly having another pair of slippers was too high for me, I could not attain unto it. I concluded that God has all the answers, and all I had to do was "Go" when He said so. Whether or not I know the results, He always makes the way if I proceed forward in faith. She looks at me and laughs when I asked her for a pair of slippers. I did not quite know what that laughter was all about, but I laugh right back. All I know was that when I laugh my blessings are released. "Yes," she said, I have one more left, but it is my vacation slippers, so please bring it back. This time, although she was laughing, she was serious, I rejoiced in the Lord, and said, "Yes Mama." I promise I would give it back. I just wonder at God at God's doing and His favor towards me.

Finally, it was a delight to be on my way downtown Newark, I was incredibly happy as I travel. I prayed and worshiped God. But there was another surprise for me when I approach my destination. My trip was not without obstacles there were street blocks from Market and Ferry Street, they were having a parade. And I simply turned and asked the Lord in a faithful manner, "Why did you send me if you know they were having a parade. Is this a test?" "Or am I to just turn back now?" After God as brought me this far with His goods. Surely, I console myself and said," After all God's planning for me today it will not go in vain." Therefore, I press my way onto victory. I may not have the answer, but I KNEW GOD GOT IT. God knew how determine I was and all I had to do was wait on Him. Because He as a way of escape for me. As the Word of God says, He always makes a way of escape for you. "The Lord told me to keep going," He told me to make a left and pull over to the side." Finally, he told me to feed His children from the jeep.

To put it briefly, I remember He had blessed me to do that a while back when I was in another dilemma and persistent on feeding my children. I certainly did not have any recollection of it until now. I followed God's instruction, and then call one of my children, to go; and call the rest, while I stayed in the jeep. I waited patiently and prayed for God's protections on them and myself. They were so grateful to see me but very surprise, they did know that I drive because I have always parked my jeep and walked for years to Penn Station. One of them tease me and said are you sure you have a license for this thing? "I just kept on laughing," "To God be the glory." He is so good to me. I thanked God, I did not turn down the pretzels, he had provided. Later, when I return to the house of the Lord, the saints, who were still there waiting for evening service to begin, were surprise to see me return back so soon. They asked, how was it possible for you to return so quickly, and I told them how God made a way of escape for me even when there seems to be no way out. They all laugh! The Lord Himself was my guiding angel on this mission. The angel of the Lord, himself was my **Angel In Disguise** on the journey, because had it not been for Him who gave me excellent and splendiferous instruction who knows I would have aborted my mission. The man who gave me the pretzels was another one-off, "**God's Angels In Disguise.**"

CHAPTER 17

God's Devine Provision Through His Kitchen Angels In Disguise
7/11/16
March 31/15 1:32 p.m.

AS mentioned in previous chapters God's divine provision do not always come the way, I often expected them. Nonetheless, the plans that He has ordained for me always come to fruition. Although I always walk in a spirit of expectancy once again, on this particular Sunday, I was not anticipating feeding the needy. I have been constantly asking the Lord to feed the needy on Sundays. From past observation that is the least day they are fed, by the communities. Many saints are in worship services on Sundays. This was a daily topic I discussed with the Lord. I even brought up the subject of how the Lord (Jesus) did thing out of the ordinary, on the Sabbath day. Like healing the sick. The Bibles tells of a man in the sanctuary with a withered hand. Jesus notice it as He was teaching and told him to stretch out his hand and it was restored. "And behold, there was a man which had *his* hand withered. And they asked him, saying, is it lawful to heal on the Sabbath days? that they might accuse him." (Matthew 12:10). I remind God that few commuters travel through Penn. Station on Sundays. The needy need to be fed as well on Sundays. Well, God did not respond to my petition as I thought. As far as I was concern, my day was ended. I was heading home to rest after church, but King Jesus had

And he shall set the sheep on his right hand, but the goats on the left.

Then shall the King say unto them on his right hand, Come, ye blessed of my Father, inherit the kingdom prepared for you from the foundation of the world:

For I was an hungred, and ye gave me meat: I was thirsty, and ye gave me drink: I was a stranger, and ye took me in:

Naked, and ye clothed me: I was sick, and ye visited me: I was in prison, and ye came unto me.

a surprise planned for me. After service, there was a special dinner prepared for a building fund. I had already eaten and was about to leave the building. When one of the evangelists called me. "She informed me that there was a pot of rice left in the kitchen and it could be used for the needy." I stop dead in my tracks, looked at her and smiled. Then asked, "Her if she was putting me to work?" "She laughed." I wonder if she had been ease dropping on my conversations with God or was God up to His old tricks again. He knows, me so well that I am faithful to Him. If He makes the provision, I will go at once and deliver. The challenge was on, it was a great idea to feed the needy. She was right, but she mentioned there was no chicken. "I replied to the Lord in my heart." "I need some meat." **I DID NOT WANT TO LEAVE THE RICE FOR ANOTHER DAY**. I reiterate to the Lord again, "that I like to distribute the food right away. Over the years, God as taught me how to expedite His task and I have learned that the "Master service requires haste." My burden is always lighter (when I follow God). As I smiled and hummed a song waiting for God's reply because I knew Him as my Jehovah Jireh. (My provider).

Geneses says: 22: 8- 15

And Abraham said, my son, God will provide himself a lamb for a burnt offering: so, they went both of them together. And they came to the place which God had told him off, and Abraham built an altar there, and laid the wood in order, and bound Isaac his son, and laid him on the altar upon the wood. And Abraham stretched forth his hand and took the knife to slay his son. And the angel of the LORD called unto him out of heaven, and said, Abraham, Abraham: and he said, here am I. And he said, lay not thine hand upon the lad, neither do thou anything unto him: for now, I know that thou fearest God, seeing thou hast not withheld thy son, thine only son from me. And Abraham lifted up his eyes, and looked, and behold behind him a ram caught in a thicket by his horns: and Abraham went and took the ram and offered him up for a burnt-offering instead of his son. And Abraham called the name of that place Jehovah-Jireh: as it is said to this day, In the mount of the LORD it shall be seen (22: 8- 15).

God has been telling me lately these encouraging word "God's got it." I Repeat when situation and decision come my way. Which simple means, He will work it all out for me. If I only trust Him. As the bible notes lean not on to your own understanding but in all your ways acknowledge Him and He will direct your path. This tells me not to worry about what is God's concern, because I know that I am His responsibility. I was to do what **I CAN, AND HE WILL DO THE REST. HE IS MY SUSTAINER, DADDY, HUSBAND, AND MY PROVIDER.** Fortunately, I am maturing and learning to leave it all in God's hands. I remember one day, while at Rutgers University. I was stressing myself out about an assignment, I had done. For some reason or another, I had lost it. I could not believe it! When I went to pull it up! It was not saved on my flash drive. I was so unhappy because it was due that morning. As I walked on the grassy campus, talking to the Lord about my problem, His response was, "Don't be uptight about it." I thought, did I hear clearly. Or was my mind playing tricks on me. God repeated it again! Without a doubt that was exactly what the Lord said. I felt so bad because I was complaining and not trusting Him. I confessed to one of my colleagues, shortly after and told her what the Lord told me, when she was complaining about her classes and how the professor was unfair. I knew God wanted her to be reassured that He can rectify the problems she faces in school. After I encourage her in the Lord. I apologize to God, prayed, and asked for His forgiveness. I asked, "Him if He could bless me with another day to turn in my assignment, and I went and explain to my professor, what happened to my assignment. Thank God! He spoke and I repented because my professor was so happy to grant me my request. The lesson I learned from my experience was that the Almighty God was bigger than my itty-bitty problems. At that moment, another missionary in the kitchen interrupted my thoughts and said, "There was a pot of gravy available." I laugh in my heart with God" and said, "I still cannot go with that alone I needed some meat please." "I laugh with the Lord because I knew he was up to something BIG, and special for His children." I was having fun with God, and "Reminded Him again in my heart that He knows me best, and I like to get things done right away, and not procrastinate. Or else it becomes a burden to me, at times, the consequence can be inadequate, and GOD knows." I knew I had gotten through to the Lord, because finally, another sister said, "Sister Marie here is a pan of chicken." I proclaim, "What chicken!" "Did you say?" "You had chicken for me? "They all laugh." Well, I jumped up and down in the kitchen and laugh." "God had come through for me using His **Kitchen Angels**" They had overlooked a batch of chicken and it was just sitting there. "Just waiting there to bless me." God certainly hid the chicken well, because the saints kept saying they were out of chicken, to the saints who wanted chicken with their meals. It was an honest mistake on their part, but God was in the midst of it.

Thank God, I was blessed to have the kitchen angel staff, who worked in the kitchen because they helped me packed the food. Thank God for His mighty host of angels who He imparts into my life to do His work.

Psalm 103 reads, "Bless the LORD, all his angel "Bless the Lord, O he angels, you mighty ones who do his word! Bless the Lord all he hosts, his ministers, who do his work. Bless the Lord, all his works, in all places of his dominion. Bless the Lord, O my soul! (103, 20-22)

I began to sing the song, "God is good, God is good to me, and how can I let him down." He so good to me." God was right He got it! It took faith for me to get what God had for me, as the Bible says without faith it is impossible for me to please God. "Faith without works is dead." I can relate to the woman in the Bible who kept going back to the mean judge, to get what belong to her.

According to Gateway Bible.com Luke 18

"And he spake a parable unto them to this end, that men ought always to pray, and not to faint; Saying, there was in a city a judge, which feared not God, neither regarded man: And there was a widow in that city; and she came unto him, saying, Avenge me of mine adversary. And he would not for a while: but afterward, he said within himself, Though I fear not God, nor regard man; Yet because this widow troubleth me, I will avenge her lest by her continual coming she weary me. And the Lord said, Hear what the unjust judge saith. And shall not God avenge his own elect, which cries day and night unto him, though he bears long with them? I tell you that he will avenge them speedily. Nevertheless, when the Son of man cometh, shall he find faith on the earth?" (Luke: 18 1-8).

In cases like these, I just use her example with perseverance by going back to the Lord with my case until He gives me justice. He got the answerers and as set goals for me, as the Bible says faith without works is dead. If I want what God has for me badly enough nothing should stop or hinder me from aspiring for it. It just takes determination. But there is an adversary Satan who do not want me to succeed. But thank God for His **Angels In Disguise,** in this story and when He says no weapon formed against me shall prosper, He really means no devices in the spiritual realm of the enemy cannot harm me.

CHAPTER 18

A Long-Lost Friend
September 6/09 7:00 p.m.

It has truly been a week of harvest for me. I have gone downtown Newark, just about every day last week. After years of fasting and deep intercessory prayers for my children, God as open doors and given them many opportunities, to relocate to better homes as well as jobs. The testimonies that they shared with me was exuberant and reflect the excellence of God's handy work, there was no doubt in my mind that it was God's doing. He had seen his children pain and suffering and grant me my heart's desire for them to have a better opportunity of living. For example, one of the homeless man, name Salem, told me about an apartment that he was getting. I was excited and told him that I had been praying for him. Instantly, he said he knows, because everywhere he went for help something good happened to him. Although I usually pray with my children outside of Penn station, it was my constant petition to God in my daily devotion for them to have a roof over their heads.

It was truly an awesome blessing for me to hear this good news. The sovereign God was turning around their situation. It was really happening, what the Lord had spoken to my spirit, as I sat in Holy Convocation, Thursday night. I can remember the Lord telling me that, "all I had prayed and asked him for was going to happen." After feeding my children, ministering to them, and taking the picture. I did not leave down town Newark, until 10:00 Pm that night because so many other accounts led up

Matthew 36-38

But when he saw the multitudes, he was moved with compassion on them, because they fainted, and were scattered abroad, as sheep having no shepherd.

Then saith he unto his disciples, The harvest truly is plenteous, but the labourers are few.

Pray ye therefore the Lord of the harvest, that he will send forth labourers into his harvest.

to me being late. After my children went back inside Penn Station when I turned around and noticed a slender Hispanic man with a few others looking around with boxes. Eventually, he came over and asked me if I know where he could find the needy because he had food for them. I was ecstatic, and I told Salem, who I was talking to at the time, to call the others inside. It was then that I really noticed that God was manifesting my request to Him by allowing me to be an eyewitness to this event. This was extremely good because more help was always needed. God always sends laborers when the harvest is ripe.

According to the Holy Bible Matthew 9 says:

> But when he saw the multitudes, he was moved with compassion on them, because they fainted, and were scattered abroad, as sheep having no shepherd. Then saith he unto his disciples, the truly is plenteous, but the laborers are few; Pray ye, therefore, the Lord of the harvest, that he will send forth laborers into his harvest." (Matthew 36-38)

I was not about to leave now I wanted to see what my Daddy was up to tonight. Filled with excitement and gratitude, I introduce myself to the gentleman and told him that I had just finished feeding them as well. The man repeated again with a smile, and said, "He had food for them." God was on the job, again I thank the Lord for sending me more help from other ministries because the need was so great. This brought great pleasure to my soul to see the church in action, eventually, I asked if I could take, their pictures as well, and, "He say yes." Therefore, I followed has he and his crew feed the needy and took their pictures. Overall, we all took plenty of pictures together. It was a pleasure to have met some of my fellow brethren in Christ.

I was on fire, as I realized God had truly answered my prayer and send out more labors in the field. I just could not get enough of what was occurring right in front of my eyes. After they finished passing out the food, I got an opportunity to speak with the leader of the team.

Although I had spoken to one of the team members earlier, I wanted to confirm that it was really God's answer to my prayer. So, I asked him if he been here before and he replied with a deep Hispanic accent "Ho no!" "Tonight, is our first night out." "Our ministry just started this mission to feed the needy" Oh, boy did I rejoiced. I told him, I had prayed and asked God to send me help! Like Nehemiah, I was doing a good work and will not come down the needy needed help and praying to Jesus was my solution. Glory! Definitely, God as opened my spiritual eyes wider to behold this wonder, He was doing, and all the glory belongs to Him! Another supernatural thing happened, while I was talking to him, a man came over to me, and said I know you. I was puzzled and began to think! He looked me right in my eyes again and insist he knew me "I immediately prayed to the Lord for help, but no answer." I could not recall his name, but I recognize his face. I felt so awkward not remembering his name, and he was so happy smiling at me. I was certain that I knew him as well. With a smile, he asked again "You don't remember me, do you?"

Finally, I responded regrettably, I know your face, but I do not recall your name because something about you has changed. Still, surprise at my lack of memory; I asked him to remind me, who, he was. His name was Victor. What a surprise! When he reveals his identity, God must have been listening to my heart cries. It was a long-lost friend of mine. I often thought about what as happen to him and his other friend James. At times, I question God about Victor and James whom, I met seven years ago while attending to the needy downtown, Newark. I was curious as to their where about and if James was still serving the Lord. After witnessing to both of them when we first met a few years ago about Jesus's love for them; they came and fellowship with us at Gospel Light Church. Eventually, James was baptized at our ministry, but Victor did not. It was certainly a pleasure to see him again. We hugged each other, with gladness and talked for a while, James informed me that Victor relocated to another state. I witness to James again about God, and the importance of him giving his life to the Lord. He wanted to know how I was doing as well as he was surprised to see me still tending to the flocks. I Thank God for the team of **God's Angels In Disguise** *who fed the needy that wonderful night. The Lord was doing so many angelic activities that night I was in awe of Him.*

CHAPTER **19**

An Exceptional Day
February 3/09 12: p.m.

The day started out with feeding the less fortunate at our church community outreach and to me, this was going to be an exceptional day in the Lord. The saints cooked plenty of delicious foods and prepared beverages. As the day progress forward the saint assist adults, and children with clothes, shoes, coats, scarf, and toys. I was on fire; for God and my, Bishop gave me permission to get some of my children, from downtown Newark to attend the community outreach. The day was exceptional, and it was a tremendous blessing, because men, as well as women from the surrounding shelters in our community, came out to hear God's word of encouragement and were fed. They were also invited to church on Sunday. After many hours of enlightening with the saints of God, and our neighbors, I had to return my other friends downtown Newark. However, my heart was broken for those that did not came to the community outreach. So, I went and asked the kitchen staff it there was any more food left over; to take with us downtown to feed the others. We were given plenty of food and clothes to take with us.

I went downtown Newark, with two of my sisters and their children. After we dropped off the souls, we brought up earlier, then we proceeded to feed the needy and of course, we ran out of food. We had to get into action and called the church for more food. It was astonishing to think that all the food we brought was gone in minutes. Where so many people came from, I did not know. I was lost for words! There were still one hundred souls to be fed this was truly an evening we would never forget. Even though, I told the people to go back inside because it was extremely cold. They insisted on waiting in the cold, I had to beg

Hebrew 2, 6 v 7

And again, when he bringeth in the first begotten into the world, he saith, And let all the angels of God worship him. And of the angels he saith, Who maketh his angel's spirit, and his ministers a flame of fire.

them to go in and assure everyone the food would come, but it would take a while. We were **God's Angels In Disguise**," and we occupied ourselves by ministering to them in songs. *When the food arrived, we were having intercessory prayer and God did* **MIRACLES SO THE FOOD MULTIPLIED**. As the Bible says God created the angels to worship His Son Jesus Christ has, he was ushered into this world and likewise He used them to minister to the needs of others. *According to Hebrew 2, "And again, when he bringeth in the first-begotten into the world, he saith, and let all the angels of God* worship him. And of the angels he saith, who maketh his angel's spirit, and his ministers a flame of fire" (6, 7).

CHAPTER **20**

An Amazing Adventure
January 19/18 6:p.m.

Last evening, was an amazing adventure for me! Given the circumstances, what began as a trying, and testing morning quickly turned into victory. Although I appreciate, my car often times for years, in the wintertime it took up to 20 minutes to warm. I often wish I had a remote-control starter to start it in the morning; while I shower, worship God, and got dress. I often talk to God about it, hoping He would provide me with a better job so I could purchase a new car with a starter or bless me with another car that has a starter. Actually, I knew God would grant me my heart's desire because I just believe Him with my whole heart. I was just waiting for God to manifest the appointed time. Of course, this morning was one of those below 0-temperature day. The Holy Ghost instructed me to go downstairs and start the car before I showered; I said, "Ok Lord!" Right away, I went downstairs with radical faith in God believing the car would start. It was freezing outside, and I was shivering. One can only imagine my shock when the car failed to start, not once, but twice when I turned

Matthew 9 36-38

And Jesus answering said, A certain man went down from Jerusalem to Jericho, and fell among thieves, which stripped him of his raiment, and wounded him, and departed, leaving him half dead.

31 And by chance there came down a certain priest that way: and when he saw him, he passed by on the other side.

32 And likewise a Levite, when he was at the place, came and looked on him, and passed by on the other side.

33 But a certain Samaritan, as he journeyed, came where he was: and when he saw him, he had compassion on him,

34 And went to him, and bound up his wounds, pouring in oil and wine, and set him on his own beast, and brought him to an inn, and took care of him.

the key in the ignition. I did not have time to question, God as to why the car refused start since He had told me to go and do so. My level of expectation from God was high and why should I doubt Him. It was early in the morning, and still dark outside, I look up in the sky and said to the Lord smiling "Where is my help"? All that was on my mind was that I have to get to college; I had a major test that afternoon and had to turn in my lab report. I lift up my car hood with the expectation that help would soon arrive.

Right at that moment, I noticed a white Verizon van coming down the street approaching me, I said, "thank you, Lord, for my deliverance". I prayed and asked the angel of the Lord to go before me. As I reach the white van with the red stripes a nice young man greeted me, I explained my situation to him and asked him to help me. He turned to me with a sad countenance and said, "I don't have a jumper cable." "I smiled backed at him, and said I have one."

Actually, it was just last week Saturday, the Lord told me to go and buy one from Sears, on my way from class. That evening, I really did not see the need to purchase one, because I was not in need. Nonetheless, I was thankful I was obedient. Even though I really did not have the money to spear, I knew obedience is better than sacrifice. In no time, he hooked the jumper cable up to my car, has he hooked up the cable to his van I took the opportunity to start up a conversation with him about the love of God. In a few minutes, my car began to run like a charm. I told him how much I appreciate it and that he had just blessed me to get to my class on time. As he drove off, I called out to him "God bless you" and have a blessed day. I knew that he was one of "**God's Angels in Disguise.**" I thank the Lord, for blessing me for being obedient to his voice. And for preparing me in advance for what was unknown to me but known to him. I recognize that God knows all things and without His direction and help, I am lost because He is a Sovereign God.

On my way home, from class that evening, I had to pick up a friend to assist me with feeding the needy. It was a challenge, but I had promised her that I would come and get her directly after school. I asked her to please be outside by 6:00 PM. To my surprise, things did not go has planned. I stopped at home to pick up something that was vital to our mission. After trying to call her on my cell phone with no success, I wonder where she was. It was only after I was in my apartment that we made contact. I had totally forgotten that she was to be outside by 6:00pm. She was a real gem patiently waiting for me outside the whole time. On that note, I ran out the house and got in the car to pick her up. Eventually, when I got there, she was practically lost on the sidewalk among an enormous number of bags filled with clothes for the less fortunate. It was a joke, because there was only space for two bags and I specifically told her to bring only two bags. I sat in the jeep and had a good laugh. The trunk was practically full of the many bags I had. I only estimate room for two more. Moreover, while on my way over; I mentioned to the Lord that I hope she remembers to bring only two bags because my trunk was already full. We greeted each other, and still laughing I said to her where are we going to put all those things. Surely, I was happy she brought the bags because there were many people in need it would not go to waste; but I needed some quick wisdom to pack it all. I cried out to the Lord, "In my heart for help!"

And of course, God blessed us to fit all the bags, except for two small ones which we left behind for another day. As a result, there was a small space left in the trunk and we decided to leave it. While on our way, my friend asked if we could make a stop at the store because she needed a space heater. She explained that her house was still cold, although her heat was on, it was not circulating properly. What and awesome God we served, the small spot we save was for her to put the heater she brought. God surely looks out for all of his children's oh Hallelujah. Here we were thinking about the poor and needy and God was setting us up for a blessing. We prayed, as we journey downtown Newark, and give God the Glory. When we reached Newark, Pen Station I had to drop my friend of and find a parking. I asked the Lord to bless me with a quick parking close to Penn Station area because it is was so difficult to get parking. I did not want to return too late and miss handing out the donations with my friend.

Needless to say, I was in for a great big surprise that day, after parking and hurrying back towards Penn station; I saw a young man falling from a distance onto a fence and finally onto the sidewalk! I ran toward him terrified he had hit his head and got a concussion. Not sure, whether he was high on drugs or drunk! Because this type of occurrences does happen often where you would often see young men and women walking and staggering on the sidewalk. At times in the streets and tipping over as they move because they are hooked on substances. It is only the grace of Almighty God; why motorist does not kill them. I prayed in my heart to God to send help. As I got closer, I called out to him and he was not responsive. He appears to be of Spanish origin. His eyes were turning over. I was frantic because he needed medical attention right away. I looked around for help and it was then that I saw a Spanish couple approaching. I told them to try talking to him in Spanish because; maybe he does not speak English.

So, they tried, as I reach for my cell phone in my coat pocket it was apparent that I left it in the car. It was no use he did not reply to their voices. I asked them to call 911 while I continue to pray to the Lord for help. It seemed like a lifetime, had passed while we waited for the ambulance to come in the

we tried to get the young man to respond but he was slump down. I kept in constant prayer asking God to speed up the ambulance because I realized this was an urgent situation. I just could not quit, so I began to persevere in prayer again until I felt a shift in the spirit. Eventually, I felt the release and that it was well and all I had to do was just trust God. I knew that God heard my prayers and was turning around the situation because the Holy Ghost was turning me around in the spirit. I felt the release again and knew the breakthrough I had prayed for was coming, but not from the ambulance, God had done the work himself. Before long, we watch has the young man got up all by himself. We looked at each other with awe and wonder. I was curious has to what is name was, and if he was all right. My new friend Julia and Roberto interpret my questions to him. He was confused as to who we were and why we were staring at him so intensely. He spoke only Spanish, and his name was Eddie. "He did not know what had happened to him, and where he was." "He was even reluctant to answer some of our questions, because he did not know us, and was afraid," I told Roberto to tell him what happened to him, who we were, and that we just wanted to help him.

May I remind you readers it was freezing cold and windy outside. It was only after Eddie's recovery that I remember how cold I was. Julia and Roberto agreed with me that they too were extremely cold! It was as if God had taken the feelings of being cold away from us until now. Yet, still, the ambulance had not arrived. We started to question each other about what is taking the ambulance so long. Then Julia told us, what the operator had said, "If Eddie had gotten any worst to call them back" so I said, "Gotten any worst he was out like a light." "What did she mean any worst?" "He was unconscious when you made the call." "What if God had not blessed Eddie to regain consciousness after he had fallen down and hit his head on the pavement? "What if God was to say to us when we call him for help to call back when our problems get worst?" "And we all laughed." By this time, Eddie was much more alert and aware of his surroundings. He wanted to go home and told us he just lives around the corner. Of course, we did encourage him to wait for the ambulance, because they were on their way. At first, Eddie said," Yes, he would wait, then changed his mind" We tried to convince him once again to wait but could not stop him. He began to walk toward Ferry Street, and we followed him and kept a close watched on each step he took just to make sure he was all right. Eventually, Eddie was out of our sight.

Julia, who was fascinated with how the power of the Holy Ghost, worked through me wanted to know where I went to church, I told her "Gospel Light." We hugged each other and exchange numbers. Julia and Roberto did not live in Newark, New Jersey. In fact, they were on their way to catch a train into New York City. By the way, did I mention they were coming from a church across the street, and Eddie had a Spanish Bible with him when he fell down? Even though he said, "he was not coming from the church. God send help and they came just in time. I thank God for His two strangers that He sent along that night to assist me with Eddie's distress. Who was a lonely traveler in need of a prayer and a helping hand. Was he one of **"God's Angels In Disguise?"**

According to Luke 10:

"And Jesus answering said, A certain man went down from Jerusalem to Jericho, and fell among thieves, which stripped him of his raiment, and wounded him, and departed, leaving him half dead. And by chance there came down a certain priest that way: and when he saw him, he passed by on the other side. And likewise, a Levite, when he was at the place, came and looked on him, and passed by on the other side. But a certain Samaritan, as he journeyed, came where he was: and when he saw him, he had compassion on him, and went to him, and bound up his wounds, pouring in oil and wine, and set him on his own beast, and brought him to an inn, and took care of him" (Luke: 30-34). God wants us to love others and do unto them has we would want for ourselves.

CHAPTER **21**

Thomas the Angel
September 28, 2009 8:14 PM

MY day started out with a ray of sunshine, and once again I WAS RUSHING OFF FOR COMMUNITY BASE CORRECTIONS CLASS. My car was so wet when I opened my car door, the driver's
seat was wet from the rained that had fallen the night before. This has been an ongoing event, but I had decided that it would not be an obstacle in my way. For some reason, the jeep just began to leak whenever it rains, and I could not figure out exactly where it was coming from. Some days, I had to bail out buckets of water from the jeep. It was only by God's grace and mercies why the jeep started. I tried several times to get a mechanic to look at it, but that just did not work out, and money was tight. Eventually, I figure out that the leaking was coming from around the sunroof. I went to Home Depot and purchase a product that was supposed to stop leaks after one of my classmate's, told me she had a similar issue and it worked for her. Yet it did not work. However, I DROVE THE JEEP TO CLASS, WET OR NOT. I always placed a plastic bag on the car seat, with a large towel and sat down on it, before I prayed for divine intervention. This morning I had only a few minutes to get to class. I was running late. Due to the fact that I WENT

Matthew25: 33-36

And he shall set the sheep on his right hand, but the goats on the left.

Then shall the King say unto them on his right hand, Come, ye blessed of my Father, inherit the kingdom prepared for you from the foundation of the world:

For I was an hungred, and ye gave me meat: I was thirsty, and ye gave me drink: I was a stranger, and ye took me in:

Naked, and ye clothed me: I was sick, and ye visited me: I was in prison, and ye came unto me.

TO BED LATE. We HAD CHURCH EARLIER THAT EVENING AND I STAYED UP LATE DOING HOMEWORK. Therefore, I asked God in advance to please pardon my lack of participation in class that morning. I was not quite pleased with my studies and was not sure I understood it, even though I did my homework. On the contrary, once our professor began the class discussion, I got the understanding and I was able to participate. It was good, thank God! After class, I WAS ON MY WAY TO THE LEARNING CENTER AT LEAST THAT'S WHAT I THOUGHT. THE LORD REDIRECTED MY STEPS AND LED ME TO THE ADMISSIONS OFFICE TO FILL OUT A SLIP FOR MY TRANSCRIPT TO SETON HALL UNIVERSITY. I WAS ACCEPTED THERE AND HAD TO HAVE THE ESSEX COUNTY COLLEGE FORWARD MY TRANSCRIPT THERE. Therefore, I follow God's leading and it was successful. Then I was off to the learning center to have my criminology research paper proofread.

After accomplishing that task, I was torn between going to church to pray or the unemployment office located in East Orange. Being in prayer at God's house has been a consistent practice for me. After I was baptized God drew me aside to spend time in prayer, in His house in the mornings. It was a marvelous blessing to me. It strengthens me spiritually, teaches me how to listen to God's voice, receives directions, and answers to my prayers. Prayer helped me to grow in God, increase faith and focus on God. It also helps me to be patient with GOD, myself, and others, which was not always easy for me. It also teaches me how to be a problem solver, and how to wait on God. It kept me at peace with God and myself. One of my main purpose to pray was for others and situations that arrive in life. Prayers were offered up in God's sanctuary to draw souls to His kingdom as well as help to bless others' lives. Most importantly, intercessory prayers were made for the spiritual growth of our ministry at Gospel Light Church. Prayer was the center of my life and a passion that kept me happy and honored to have such a close relationship with "My Lord." This was just one of the many glorious things, God had placed in my heart to do over the years. Moreover, it has given me a closer walk and passion for God. So, I asked the Lord, what shall I do, and He replies, "Go and pray." I am happy I did ask! I do not like to be in the wrong place at the wrong time it is very time-consuming. As I finished my prayer, My Pastor came. I had plenty of homework to do. Another assignment I had forgotten until now was to prepare food to feed the needy. It was the Lord who reminded me, and "I said yes Lord."

According to Psalms 41:

> Blessed is he that considereth the poor: the LORD will deliver him in the time of trouble. The LORD will preserve him, and keep him alive, and he shall be blessed upon the earth: and thou wilt not delivers him unto the will of his enemies. The LORD will strengthen him upon the bed of languishing: thou wilt makes all his bed in his sickness (41; 1-30).

In no time, I had the food prepared and was on my merry way. My Pastor, his wife, and one of our sister's in Christ wished me all the best. I knew they would be praying for my safety. It was after 2 pm, I had been fasting, and the bags were heavy, so I sat in the car for a while. An officer came by handing out parking tickets, and I asked him if where I parked was ok, He said, "Only four hours parking is permitted." I am never sure about those parking sign so, I thank God, he delayed me, so I could know the facts about the hours of parking. Once again, I was on my way with my cart to feed God's children.

When I arrived, a gentleman greeted me and asked, "Where do I attend church." He wanted the address, so he could visit and, I told him. I presume this was "**God's Angel In Disguise**". "Was God just checking up on me in the field?" As I meditate on these thoughts, I head toward the benches that I usually place the food bags on. Afterwards, I heard someone yelling "Marie". It was Thomas my friend calling me, he came over to greet me, while the others were being fed online. In a few minutes all, the food was gone.

Thomas drew me aside and gave me some sad news, which grieves my spirit, and I felt extremely sad! One of my children had died that morning; I began to communicate with the Lord about this

. His name was Casey he was born in Haiti, HE WAS EXTREMELY tall, and IN HIS LATE FIFTIES. He was kind, with a few of his front teeth missing when he smiled. He too was one of my valuable second helper who assists with feeding the needy, when I was short staff. Casey's biggest problem was that he was an alcoholic and it was hard for him to kick the habit, but when he was not drinking, he was one of the nicest people on the face of the earth. No matter how much I told him about the Lord, he was reluctant to give his life to the Lord. I was thinking these through to God wondering if God had mercy on him and he made it to heaven. I always prayed for him; my sadness was because I do not know where his soul went!

Finally, I got back to reality and asked Thomas if he was sure? And he said, "Yes." One of the police officers told him when he got off the train this morning.

In conclusion, my problem with the jeep was not yet solved, it was summer, and heavy rain was still pouring just about every day. I even use plastic bags to cover my jeep after I could not locate a jeep covering in the stores, just to avoid the rain from getting in. When I parked my jeep, it looks really crazy with the black garbage bag I place on it with big rocks and tape to keep it down. God was too outrageously funny, he sends the rain that came with the wind and it would somehow blow the plastic off the jeep, and I was back to bailing out water. "I thought to myself how God could continue to send me so much rain?" "He sees and knows how much it was affecting me." "Is He funny are what?" In response, "I just began to laugh with God and thank Him every time it rains; and the jeep was flooded with water." I began to laugh with Him as well when I was driving, and the rain began to pour in the jeep. At times, "I did wonder would God ever stop the rain." "What was He teaching me" "Was I too uptight again" Or He was just trying to tell me He was in control. "As well as make me laugh because He is so humorous."

I knew God was with me because He always blesses the jeep to start despite the amount of water that would accumulate in the jeep and stay there overnight. God never let me down. Nonetheless, one day after petitioning God again about my problem the minister who helped me purchase the jeep call to check up on me. He also asked how the jeep was running and I told him. He not only fixed the sunroof but suction out all the water that was in it. He works so diligently on it, one would think it was his jeep It was just the magnificent help of this angel the Lord sent to help me, that keep me during that season of my life.

When I finally got it to the mechanic, he was perturbed as to how the jeep was still running and I was not shocked to death, due to the severity of the water flooding, and damage it had been through. Clearly had I not have the fear of the Lord inside my heart, I would not have been delivered from my circumstances. As Psalms 34: 7 rightly states, "The angels of the Lord encamped round about them that fear him and delivered them".

CHAPTER 22

"THE ANGELS ARE HERE" "THE ANGELS ARE HERE"
December 12/16 9:30 p.m.

It all began when my surgery was canceled for Robotic Laparoscopic Myomectomy to remove 2 fibroids from my uterus. I was home on what was supposed to be a disability leave. Yet, due to the cancellation, I was home with my cat Glory and time on my hands and still could not return to work and my disability was on hold. Before, the appointed time of my surgery, I tried to find Glory a place to stay. However, it was a hard task to find him a cat sitter. But when I did, they were genuinely nice to Glory. They were a couple who ran a private shelter for homeless cats in Scotch Plains called, "H.A.R.P. which is connected to Pet Smart. They came to my house the day before my scheduled operation to get Glory. I was speechless at their passion and compassion for Glory, especially the husband. They offered to visit him in my apartment twice a day and feed him until I return from the hospital. Also, after my surgery, they would continue to take care of him till I was well. But I told them it would not be possible because the doctor said I could not climb the stairs for weeks. And also, it would be best for them to take him with them because it would be too much for me. Glory wakes up 5 am, every morning to be fed and I do not expect them to come here that early. I often tell Glory he needs to pray to God, because of his early morning schedule. In the upcoming events will show why Glory had an operation instead of me. Who can understand the Almighty God we serve? Yet, according to the Bible God is able to do exceedingly and abundantly above all I could ever think or ask of Him if I just trust Him. While the couple was heading back home with Glory the wife called to asked me about Glory's medical history. She wanted to know if he was updated on his 2 shots. "I told her no." I knew what God was up to when she called and inquired about Glory's shots. It had been my prayer for

> HE WILL GIVE HIS ANGELS CHARGE OVER US TO KEEP US IN ALL OUR WAYS (91).

him to be updated on his shots. Yet I could not afford to pay for it. Jennifer offered to pay for them. I was bursting with glee. Too excited for words. I said yes thank you! Jennifer starts to explain the process and that she would take him to a veterinarian. I told her to go right ahead. Who am I to stand in God's way when He is blessing me? When I hung up the phone I was screaming and shouting "You did it" that was a part of the reason I told them to take Glory because God told me to let them take him. I knew He was up to something big. I needed a break from my cat. All I wanted was time alone with Jesus and I had told this to Him. That evening and the following morning was like heaven to me. No Glory, to pat me on my cheek at 5 am. Or sit on top of me. I was enjoying Jesus. Especially for the preparation given to me by the nurses at the hospital, which was to be done the evening as well as the following morning for surgery, my cat is too nosey. I wanted peace, quiet time with God without interruptions. But as I mentioned in the first paragraph the following morning at the hospital my operation was canceled.

The following day I called Jenifer and let her know, but she called me back later and asked if she could neuter Glory. As the Lord sometimes say to me "the best is yet to come." I had to put the phone close to my ears just to make sure I was hearing right. Jenifer loves to explain about cats and what is good for them. I learned so much from her about cats. What she did not know was that God had told me to spade- neuter Glory for a long time now. I told Him what if Glory wants to get married and have kittens in the future when He gives me a home? God was right I did not want Glory to have the surgery and yes, I did not have the money. However, I did some research on it. Yes, I told God how costly it was. The main reason God was giving me this blessing was that male cat's urine smells extremely high. My apartment is small and though I clean Glory's litter box 3-4 times a week it still leaves an odor in the house. So, guess what readers when we do not trust God enough, He as a way of having His own way because His will must be done in our lives. Now, when I realized what God was up to, I said yes to her. She kept saying are you sure? In fact, she started to change her mind. She said she did not want to take the responsibility if anything happens to Glory during surgery. I was laughing in my heart. What devil you better let go of my blessing. She said can I send my husband over with a paper for you to sign. I consulted with Daddy Jesus, who "told me yes go ahead sign them." Within minutes he was at my gate and I ran down and sign the agreement under the anointing of Almighty God. It was sealed from the presence of GOD was flowing through me. I knew I had nothing to do but pray for Glory during the time of his operation. Well, readers hear is a part of my secret, before Glory leaves the house I bath him, anointed him, and prayed God's favor over him that where he went after he leaves my house he would be blessed. Return to me better than when he left. As Ephesians 3:20-21 says, "Now to Him who is able to do exceedingly and abundantly above all we could ever ask or think of Him." Glory was sent to me by God and I knew it. I had met his owner Elizabeth the Saturday night at Shop Rite, in East Orange. She was from Trinidad a small island in the West Indies. I was searching for inexpensive cat litter and food. Enjoying a conversation with the Lord when she interrupted and told me which was the best litter and food to purchase. I turned to her and asked if she had a cat because I was about to receive one. Elizabeth said," yes and she had more than one." I told her about a cat I was supposed to get, that the person was having problems with it. Elizabeth said I could come and get one of her kittens the following day which was Sunday. I was not sold on the idea of getting the cat on Sunday morning because I had to go to church. We were having our Holy Convocation, and I did not want to miss the conclusion. As a matter of fact, I have missed tonight's meeting just by walking by faith.

It has been months now and God had told me to get a cat to fix my rat problems at home. I had told the landlady and she had not fixed the problem. I prayed until one night I was on my way home from Rutgers-Newark campus and heard a kitten crying in the distance. As I got closer to where my car was parked 20 minutes away from the campus. I began to say, Lord, I hope he is not by my car. But I knew it was there the kitten was. Fasting and praying bring about a lot of answers one does not have to ask God He just reveals it. This revelation was not a happy one. It felt like the kitten was in my womb. I could feel the kitten's anguish. Finally, I reached the car and it was under my tire crying. I do not know how he separated from its mother. It was a fairly new kitten very pretty. I did have an argument with the Lord in the cold. How am I going to feed the kitten? I cannot even feed myself. What am I going to tell the landlady? Is the kitten going to cry? I was reluctant to bring it home. When I did make up my mind to take the cat home and got some cereal from my car trunk to feed it. The kitten ran away. I chase it but could not catch it. I repent that night and asked God to forgive me.

To this day, I felt bad because it was extremely cold outside. It is better to obey God than pay. I pay for my groceries at home every time I check all my goods were eaten even my clothes in the closet by rats. God's compassion towards me was unimaginable He always replenishes my foods stock and clothes. During the first 4 nights of convocation, the Lord led cats in my path. One night I came home after midnight and a black cat came right in front of my house door and began to roll in front of me "as if to say take me home" I laughed and said I know it is you, Lord, I am not taking him. As I enter the house because the basement door was open a rat ran across my path, I was terrified. I hated them, I stood my ground that night and had a fight with the rat to come out of the house. I open the house door and command it to go." Ultimately, one afternoon while heading to Bible teaching for convocation, I sat in the car to pray, and the Lord showed me 2 black and white kittens identical, next door to my house playing in the heat. Finally, "I said yes, Lord when I return home from Bible class, I will ask my neighbor for one." That day it was about 115 degrees in Newark. It was hot. "It feels like HELL'S FIRE as describe in the Bible." I thank God, I had a jeep. Although there was no AC in it. It boggles my mind at times how God brought me through those trying times. Upon returning home, I asked my neighbor for one of his kittens and he said yes. He explained that they were wild, but he would get one for me. In my mind, I thought it would be sad to separate the kittens. They were each other's company we agree he would bring the kitten in the evening. However, when he did not show, up that evening, I when and rang his doorbell.

I am a determine person especially when I tell God yes. I will do something. I have to follow through because I know he is depending on me. My neighbor said,

set a trap for them but they did not return to the house yet. Once in my apartment, I told God I was going to pretend the kitten was here. I took out a ball and roll it to my may believe kitten in the kitchen. I kept calling the kitten and laugh. I searched the apartment for tuna fish, bowls, and other items I believe would be essential for the kitten. Honestly, I came up with partially nothing. Which was disappointing. I simply just wanted to be prepared for the kitten.

That night I mentioned to the Lord I would go and get cat litter for the cat. I know nothing about taking care of cats. I only have $13.00. I need gas and sat in the car and asked God how was I going to buy gas and purchase the kitten's provision. I would never have gone to Shop- Rite. It is disorganized but God said to go there. It would save on gas and I would be able to get what I need for the kitten.

This is the story of how Glory came to be in my life.

When I reached the lady's house that Sunday morning I was instantly reversing backward. Not because of the state of the home, but the abundance of cats that were there and they were black. The sight of her house filled with a large cat family and an old dog, made me horrified. Yes, black cats with white stripes. She said I could have one of them but, they all came towards me. I began to pray in my heart,

"Lord help me."
"I don't want any black cat."
"Please get me out of here."
Elizabeth interrupted my prayer,
and said, "Marie come and sit on the sofa."
I said in my heart to God,
What I am not stepping a foot over there."
"What is this?"
"That's not what I was expecting."
"It really was not what I was expecting,
"but it was what God had for me."
I walk very slowly towards the sofa and sat down.
"I was scared to death."
"And wondered what's wrong with her."
"Was this a cat farm?"
Still talking to myself, "She did not tell me, she had so many kittens and cats."
"And not to mention the old dog."
"What was this all about?"

With all the questions in my heart, I sat down on the brown sofa. One thing for sure she keeps her house clean and there was no odor. Elizabeth began to tell me her story of why she had so many cats and kitten in her apartment. Her mom, like her love cats and when the cat had kitten, they would find good homes for them. It was hard for them to trust anyone with the kittens unless they knew you were honest people. If one was not pleased with the kitten, Elizabeth requires you to return it back to her. She told me to return 2 and a 1/2 which was the name she gave (Glory) because he only had 2 1/2 whiskers. In the future if I was not satisfied with him. I thought this woman was really in love with her cats. As I sat on the sofa listening to her, the entire cat family with the old dog sat in a circle facing me. They all were looking at me. I do not know what they were thinking. Maybe they were simply happy to have company. They were very well trained, but I did not want their attention. I just wanted out of there.

Elizabeth said, "Marie I have the perfect kitten for you. He is quiet and genuinely nice. There are two of them brothers, but he is incredibly quiet. Just as I prayed at home and asked God for Elizabeth confirmed. I request this of God because I was not going to tell my landlady I had a cat. So, God was in it up to His neck and was laughing at me. Especially, when I saw the black cat family. I know God knows all things and wanted to deliver me from all superstitions. From I was a child people spoke badly about black cats and associate them with evil and Halloween. But the cats are not evil it the people who are ungodly and do evil things with the cats. God taught me a lesson and deliver me from that nonsense.

Elizabeth said, "Marie there he is as she pointed to one of the kittens."

I said, "To God in my heart who told her I wanted the cat." Then another cat, move out from among the family and jump up on the sofa, sniffed my gray running skirt and then sat on me. I was scooting over not wanting the cat next to me.

Elizabeth was excited "Marie 2 and ½ loves you""

"I choose his brother for you, but he is the one for you."

"I said no."

"She said yes."

He loves you" she said, "great Lord I said in my heart a noisy cat!"

"I asked for a quiet

." But I have to listen to the Lord. I told her fine and we put the kitten in the box. She gave me instruction to get him home safely, so he does not run out the box. Without me asking Elizabeth, **"God's Angel In Disguise** "offered to assist me with 2 and ½ provision.

After he got to my house the kitten ran under the bed. I had to go outside for something in the jeep. On my way back to the house, guest who God had coming in on the driveway. Yes, my landlady. He said, "Tell her you have a kitten!" I said, "Uh!" He said, "Go and tell her?" I did and she began with all kind of negative things about cats and excuses. I just simply told her what God said, and she said ok. I went in my apartment rejoicing God had won the victory for me. As the good book says, the battle is not mine it belongs to the Lord. I acquire Glory's name through the topic of our 2012 Holy Convocation. "When the Glory of God comes, it brings about change"

Owning Glory eventually led me to feeding homeless cats and kittens in my community. The compassion I felt for these stray cats was great. I had to use Glory's food and feed them. I would always tell Glory he is feeding his cousins and one-day God would bless him back for giving to them. Glory would come out with me as I feed them or watch me from the bedroom window. My land lady's son soon began to assist me in feeding them. God was doing a new thing on my block and all the neighbors were getting involved. I began to find homes for the kittens. One of the cats has 5 kittens. God even gave me a vision of the kittens before they were born. It was amazing. Now back to why I started this chapter.

With God, all things are possible due to my issue even Glory's urine affected my health. God who is compassionated, send people to my home to take Glory for the day I was to be operated on. The Almighty God that I serve would always finds ways to bless me all I have to do was asked. In serving God I realize that He would use whatever opportunity He see at the present time in my life to bless me and my house whole. I know God is blessing me no doubt. I feel it, sense it, and expect it. God as renewed Glory's health. He slept so much and was disciplined; he slept in his bed and continue to do so. I was happy when he was gone. I love my cat, but I love God more. I enjoyed my time alone that nigh with My King Jesus. I rested in the word, fast, prayed for Glory during his time of surgery. Before he left the house, I bath him and anointed him in the name of Jesus for favor with God and with people. When Glory came home, he was a different cat. He used to cry at night and make a lot of noise, but all of that has stopped and the odor was gone from his urine. Thank God!

The couple came and rescue us again, by providing food for Glory, which was an expensive cat food, due to his urinary tract issue. I showed Papa Jesus the pantry and asked Him to provide for Glory through them and He did. They paid for his shots, operation, and food and I never left the house they came to me. Isn't God good? Romans 2 :11-16 says, "For there is no respect of person

with God." So, God uses whom He chooses to bless His children. "When there are coming to my house, I ran around the house shouting the angels are here" Glory would chase after me as I ran and shout. "The angels are here" Because if God could use a dove to help Noah during his time certainly God can do it in my time as well. They reminded me of when God visited Sara and Abraham with the other 2 angels in their home before He destroyed Sodom and Gomora. Genesis 18 reads, "And he lifts up his eyes and looked, and, lo, three men stood by him: and when he saw *them*, he ran to meet them from the tent door, and bowed himself toward the ground" (Genesis 18:2). I thought to myself would God treat me that well if it was I who was operated on. What would my beloved Daddy Jesus have done for me? What do you think about our God we serve readers?

CHAPTER 23

The ANGELS ARE HERE PART 210:41PM
January 9/17 10:41 p.m.

Not withstanding, while I was home, food was needed in the house. I said, Lord, "I know you will send someone to fill my fridge with groceries." "I opened the fridge and showed it to the Lord." "Then I clean it out and left it empty." I just wanted my basic needs to be met. I just felt the Almighty God would send me food. All I had to do was keep my spirit of expectancy high on Him. My asking was not just for me only. I had prayed plus asked, "The Omnipotent God for bread to make sandwiches for the needy." I had plenty of chicken that was given to me but no bread.

> Philippians 13: 2:1
>
> 13 For it is God which worketh in you both to will and to do of his good pleasure

About 3-days later, while working on this book as the Lord instructed me to do. My landlady called out to me, "Marie, there are giving out food on Abuginer street. That was just about 2 minutes away, it was the street next to me. I had been home for 3 weeks sick and had not told her anything. What was puzzling to me as well is she was not supposed to be home at this hour of the day. She is usually working. Only God knows why she was home and used her to bless me. What an unlikely source my Father Jesus used to bless me. Now I realize God is no respecter of person. The Bible says He will use your enemies to bless you. And sometimes when you see who God uses to bless you it puzzles your mind because He is a righteous God, He uses who he chooses. As the Bible says, God will and to do of His good pleasure. Philippians 13: 2:1 says,

"For it is God which worketh in you both to will and to do of
his good pleasure." With all this in mind, I said,
"Ok Lord." "Jump up!" And said, "Again yes Lord I am coming."
"I ran to the bathroom washed my face brush my teeth."

"This blessing cause for haste I told myself."
"I left the shower"
"It would take too long since I love to sing and worship while I shower."
"Jesus was blessing me, and a shower would definitely delay me."
"I jumped in my clothes."
"My black boots, and grabbed my hat"
Put on my coat and ran out the house."
Saying, Lord, I am coming."

This blessing was heavenly, and heavy I could sense it in my spirit. I hopped in my jeep. Drove off praising and thanking God not knowing what He had in store for me. It was literally around the corner, not even two minutes' walk. But when one is expecting from God like I do; my bare hands cannot carry the provision of blessing God's has for me. That is why I drove the jeep. Anytime I go to receive from God, I always go expecting for others not just for myself. It was a divine setup from God, as I park and enter the driveway of the lady who was distributing the food. She began to tease me that I look like someone she knows. She even called me by her name. I said I am not her and giggled. She replied, "I know you are not her" "But you look just like her." And her friend who was standing next to her said, "Yes you do." They were like old friends as I introduce myself to them.

Sonia was the name of the lady in charge and I told her my story. She said, "You will never be in need again". "Abundance for you." The anointing and presence of God were upon me is such abundance. I recall the Lord had given me the word abundance over a year ago. I wrote it down on a piece of paper and place it on my mirror in the bedroom. I would repeat it as I anoint myself and pray every morning has the Lord leads. Miraculously it happened. It was not just a promise anymore, but God was using my circumstances to fulfill His covenant.

That day I receive over 100 breads in all shape, flavor, shape, and size. And it all came from my favorite supermarket, "Trader Joe's." That was just bread, there were so many other food products. My jeep was full of food. There was no room in the front seat for a helper, and yes, I needed one. I delivered, to senior buildings, shelters, and friends it was just too much goodly godly fun for me. Who said, you cannot have fun serving JESUS? That day my strengthen started to return and healing began in my life How ironic I did not have the surgery, but God had something great planned just for me. I made two trips that day to Sonia house with the jeep, just giving away the best food products ever. "Trader Joe's." The following day there was another delivery to Sonia house, and I was a part of it. This was such fun because I enjoy sharing and giving to others. This time, I could call my uncle and a few others who were available to come and part take of this fantastic ministry. For me reaching my destination with the groceries was key. It was too much for me alone to carry in, so I was totally depending on "**God's**

Angels In Disguise," for help. As I drove alone, I prayed. When I approach the door to one of the senior residences a woman came running outside with a cart. As well as another elderly person came to assist me. I kept saying, "The angels are here, "**God's Angels In Disguise**." I did not call my friend who lived there this time, so I knew it was God's doing. It was so, as well the other day, even though I told my friend who lives there I was on my way over with groceries. Upon my arrival, 2 ladies came out and helped me. My friend was not there yet. As the Bible states, to whom much is given much is required. Eventually, when she came downstairs the food was already in the building. God specializes in the things that are impossible He can do what no other power cannot do. According to Luke 1:37 For with God nothing shall be impossible (37). As I worked for the Lord, I felt healing, strength, joy, restoration, and peace. There is so much joy in giving to others. I even gave a bag of bread to a friend of mine's neighbor and I love his attitude. He said," I am going to share it with others, "I said yes!" "That's the spirit" "That's the whole idea." God wants us to bless each other as He blesses us. The Bible says it is more blessed to give that to receive.

The next Saturday was the same thing, food, and more food. God began, to surprise me. As I worked for Him. He sends me a huge bag of kale. Not one is you buy in the supermarket it was the size of a garbage bag. I chuckled, He told me to eat kale and yes, I did obey. Nevertheless, when I could not afford it God reward me with abundance. As the scripture said, "They shall not be ashamed in the evil time: and in the days of famine, they shall be satisfied. (psalm 37:19). It continues to occur; organic yogurt was another product I need to consume and did until I could not afford it. God not only send abundance He sends me pumpkin yogurt too. This was hilarious and it was healing to my mind, body, and soul just to sit back and watched the Holy God of Israel worked it all out for me when my back was against the wall. Satan had to flee when God began to rain in my community there was just no room for the devil. I was blessed and I knew it. I kept saying,

"God is blessing me."
"Lord you are crazy about me and I know it"
"Actions speaks louder than word."
"It was obvious by God's angelic actions in my life."
"He loved me very much."
"By expressing it in an extravagant and great ways with joy to me."
And the list goes on," Ezekiel bread came, pomegranate,
brown eggs, asparagus, Brussel sprouts."

And all sorts of organic products which God told me to eat. There was just one problem I had no space for them all. I gave away so much and because the food was coming so frequently, I was not getting to eat it. I did not want to waste it. God knows how to slow down the process as well and He did. God was working it out in my favor. There was a major event approaching in our ministry, and I could not figure out how I could do the food distribution and still be on time, Yet, I was still determined to do Gods' work, and He would have to intervene and give me ingenuity. It was our Bishop and Evangelist 39 appreciation service that weekend, and my God did a marvelous thing for me. God postpone the food trucks and brought what I needed instead. "He cares about what I am going through." A pastor told me that after our 38 Holy convocation and hugged me. I was prayed for because of the fibroids in my womb I was crying at that time. Really, what I was going through at the time I really wonder if God cared about my affliction.

Besides all that food, Sonia has been saying to me, I am going to give you some coats. When I leave her presence, I would ask God, "Why is she saying she has coats for me?" I don't need any coats." "She would insist these are for you." "Don't give them away." God never answered me. As I speak with her on the phone or saw her in person, she would mention the coats again. I went back to the Lord, and asked, "Why is she always saying she has 4 coats for me?" "Where am I going to put them?" "I just have to give them away." I said, "Lord they really do not know me, even my mom gave me things in the past and said don't give it away; but I can't help myself that's just who I am." "I love to give." The Bible said, it is better to give than to receive" You Lord, "has been telling me to give." I MUST DO HAS YOU SAY!

It was only as it began to get colder and caught me off guard. I came to the knowledge of what was happening to me. Working so diligently in the food distribution ministry had kept me immensely busy and I had forgotten to prepare my winter coats. Although, I mentioned to the Lord it would be done. It slipped my mind. I am always prepared for every season of my life in advance, but this one caught me off guard. I was not able to wash or rinse-out my winter coats. Then I realized why God had told Sonia to give me the coats. It was not Sonia who was speaking to me it was God. She knew nothing of my consistent routine of preparing for the winter. Once I was aware of it, I said yes, "Lord when is she going to call me to get the coats. Let me tell you how GREAT A FATHER JESUS IS TO ME. What God did was have her canceled the food distribution this weekend and instead brought in coats just to bless me and reward me for my 'faithfulness. My Bishop's wife always tells me this, "Sister Marie you are so faithful." I never really consider myself as such. It is only through the demonstration of God's actions in my life, I can discern His faithfulness to me. So, she is right God does reward me according to my obedience to do what He tells me to do. My heart's desire is for God to bless me to be submissive to Him always, and in everything. He is worthy and deserves it. The coats came just on time for Christmas when it was bitterly cold. Abruptly, the temperature changed a few days before Christmas. Sonia called to say, I could come over for the coats. Yet, I was not conscious of her phone call and missed the message. One evening, I said, "Lord if you love me, you would send the coats now, it was freezing outside and each night it was supposed to get colder. One night I check my messages and got a message. When I hear the voice mail, the Lord told me to call her. Sonia said, with regret in her voice, "I called you for the coats and did not get you." I am leaving the house now and you will have to get them another time." It was now are never, I must go back to church tonight and I was not going without an appropriate coat. I said, "No wait". I Will be there in 2 minutes". I jumped into my clothes. I said Lord, "she really doesn't know how crazy I am." Whatever you said to do I got to do." I ran out the house like lighting and left the car. I was there in less than 2 minutes. When she saw me, she laughed? I refuse to lose God's blessings. He as for me, and it is so much fun to enjoy God tricks." And if 4 coats were not enough. Sonia gave me 2 longer coats a few days later. I said, "Lord you are my Jehovah-jireh." What have I done for You to provide so much for me? These 2 last coats were God's doing, although I was thankful for the 4 shorter ones. However, I did express to him that I would prefer a longer one to cover my legs because I always wear my skirts in the winter. JESUS is my PROVIDER. Off course, I did give some away plus the ones I own. God is really real if one allows Him to reveal Himself to them "God said, "the secret of the Lord is with them that fear Him". The healthy foods I need came just by me thinking about them, during the week and by Friday or Saturday, there were here in abundance. God is really funny because Sonia always says, "I have something for you, and she would always hold up a big bag. I would laugh because I knew it was God.

"I never told her what I wanted" "It was God I told at home or in my thoughts."

The topic for the appreciation service was "The Gift You Are." how lovely. The gift cannot expire, was what a preacher from Florida expounded on. He kept repeating God said, "The gift can't be expired." "No matter what it is yours." By Monday evening, God fulfill His words in my life. I laughed! As I called Author Learning Center, again to informed them that I desire to cancel my annual subscription. I had tried during the week and was not successful. Although I left a detailed message no one returned my call. It is amazing how God's spirit operates although I was cancelling the subscription, I could feel it all over me that, it was not God's plan in the end. The sales representative who answered the phone was from India. It was difficult to understand him, he informed me that they tried to charge my visa card, but access was denied. So, I do not have to pay until 2017. It was a gift to me. However, he said, "Since you are on the phone now you have to pay the $149.00." I said what did you say Sir, "did you just told me the gift was mine for one year and he said yes but and he repeat it all over again. You must pay since you are on the phone. I realized what was happening and began to call Daddy Jesus. The devil is a liar who God bless no man curse. I told him to cancel it, but I asked God first. Then there was another catch there was a 90-day trial that was sent to me. I told him I will take that. But make sure he cancels the other one first. Then he asked for another visa card, I said, "you said it was free" the response was I need a credit card number for you to sign up. I desire time to talk with the Lord, and at the same time, the Lord let the phone buzz on the other end. I told him to hold on. As I return to speak with him, I did as the Lord instructed me, "told him I don't have one now and would get back to him. Then the Lord told me to check my email and look at the subscription, it was still activated. Then He said to check my e-mail there was 2 e-mail a minute apart "The first one state here is your GIFT for one year" the other said your subscription canceled. The gift was mines all along. God was right the "gift can't expire." Just before Christmas God uses Sonia to bless me with 200 coats to distribute to my children downtown Newark the jeep was filled with bags. This was my heart's desire to bring them coats, but once again there were so many that my team and myself took some to the Good Will shelter in Newark. And the list goes on, Geico insurance was the next blessing God send in the mail, without me asking for it, but I knew it was on its way. It is not hard to distinguish God's action as one seeks him in prayer for others to be bless. Then my eyeglasses nightmare turned into rejoicing after I follow God instructions and call my insurance and told them about the incidence. Jesus is blessing me.

To be continued!

POEMS
I OPEN MY HEART TO THE LORD JESUS

Those who open their heart's Jesus said, I will come in and sup with them.
Open the doors of my heart Lord.
Open the doors of my heart Lord.
I want you to come in and sup with me.
Open the doors of my heart Lord Jesus.
I want you to come in and sup with you.
Lord, I open the doors of my heart to you.
So, you can come in and sup with me.

MY HUMA! MY HUMA!

Who sat me down by her side on a wooden bench while she beats coffee to sell on the streets?
My Huma! My Huma!
Who keeps a close watch on me just, so no one would harm me?
My Huma! My Huma!
So old and bent down.
Was given the great responsibly to take care of me,
When she should be spending her later years of life in a rocking chair.
My Huma My Huma
So, faithfully she waited on the Lord.
"Waiting" for her Lord and Savior Jesus to call her home.
Thank God for my Huma!

SONG
JUSTICE
2/2/15

Justice demands that I serve you, Lord
Justice demands that I serve you, Lord.
Oh, death where is your sting?
Oh, grave where is your victory?
Oh justice, oh justice.
Where is your victory?
True victory comely comes from serving You Lord.

GOD'S STEP SONG
6/19/17 11:22pm

Ever step belongs to God.
Ever step belongs to God.
Ever ear belongs to God.
Order my steps in your word Lord.
Ever ear belongs to God.
Ever joy belongs to God.
Ever joy belongs to God.
The steps of a good man are order by the Lord.
Ever love belongs to God.
Ever love belongs to God.

Ever go belongs to God.
Order my steps in your word Lord.
Ever go belongs to God.
Belongs to God.
Belongs to God.
Belongs to God.

POEM
SILENT RIVER
4/2/16

The water stood so still.
Yet, it seems to be full of life.
It seems to take deep breaths like people do.
How can it be?
Did God create water with life?
Does water really breathe?
Or is it just my imagination running wild?
As I stood by the lakes, oh, the water looks so great, and seems full of life.

SONG
YOU ARE THE ONE
6/18/17 7:24pm

You are the one I been praying for.
You are the gift I been praying for.
You are the vessel I been praying for.
You are the one.
You are my King
You are my King
Lord, you are my King.
You are the one I have been praying for.

SONG
I AM AN INSTRUMENT FOR JESUS
7:39pm

I am an instrument.
Design and preserved to show froth the GLOR-Y of God.
God said, "I am an instrument" "made for His Glory."
I am the instrument, God made me to be, to show forth His Glory.
I am an instrument for God.
To show forth His GLOR-Y
To show forth His GLOR-Y
God says," I am an instrument" an instrument.
An instrument, an instrument created to show forth His GLOR-Y.

WITH MY WHOLE HEART, I WILL SERVE YOU OH LORD
8/18/2016

Hallelujah, hallelujah hallelujah
I will praise you I will praise you I will praise you.
Oh Jesus
I will worship you I will worship you I will worship you.
Oh Jesus
I will serve you I will serve you I will serve you.
Oh Jesus
Hallelujah, hallelujah, hallelujah

I AM GOING UP WITH JESUS

I am going up with Jesus, praise the Lord.
Singing shouting, praising the Lord.
I am going up full of the Holy Ghost to be with my Lord.
I am going up to GLORY praise the Lord.
Going up, going up, praise the Lord, singing, and shouting praise the Lord.
I am going to Glory praise the Lord.
I am going to Glory, Glory, Glory praise the Lord.

JEWISH PROVERB

Every blade of grass has an angel bending over it saying," Grow, grow!"
Eileen Elias Freeman

Be an angel to someone else whenever you can, as a way of thanking God for the help of your angel!
David Connolly

Eventually you will come to your own unique
Understanding about angels
And what they mean to you.
Douglas Pagels

May your days be
All blessed
With the presence
of an angel
Watching over
you.
Exodus 23:20

Angels Blessings
Behold,
I am going
To send an angel
Before you
To guard you
Along the way.

Just chilling at the beach!

MARIE E. WILLIAMSON

As a prayer intercessor, worshiper, humanitarian worker, speaker, author radio host of "Live In The Moment! You Have Not Seen Anything Yet" and a Life and Transformational Coach. She shares real life passionate radical testimonial experiences with her clients that encourage them, so they can be spiritually transform, heal, and delivered. While guiding and counseling them through the center of their problems with the word of God because Jesus Christ is the life giver and transformer. God's word is use has a tool to enrich their religious lives as well as she use my professional administrative and versatile spiritual abilities to develop their spiritual gifts.

As the word of God says, "I can do all things through Christ which strengthens me" and this is the motto that she live by to achieve both spiritual and professional success and this scripture too can restore and transform anyone who dears to apply it to their daily life. One may ask themselves what does a spiritual transformation do? What a spiritual transformation does is bring one into an intimate relationship with Jesus Christ their Savior.

As a social reform humanitarian, she seek's to promote human welfare, her mission is to assist and encourage, the poor and needy in her community, which has been a constant goal of hers. Which has been both local and international service to God's people; her various duties have taken her too many private shelters that house men, women, and children in Newark, East Orange, and Orange.

Her work involves one on one witness, food distribution, clothing, and speaking engagements as well as distributes varieties of food products to several East Orange senior building housing as much as 300 residents. In addition, her greatest, passion in Christ is working within the field among the less fortunate who resides at Newark, Penn Station allocating food, comfort, love, counseling, and clothing.

Finally, her steady prayer and desire is for God to grand them proper homes, with stability and favor intended for an Azusa street revival, which took place on April 9, 1906 in Los Angeles County, California, United States. This revival purpose is for them to experience the power of the Holy Spirit with the intent to cause break-through, breakout, and break-forth within their destiny during this end time.

REFERENCES

Biblegateway.com
Wake up, de Blasio" author Curtis Sliwa
New York Post July 17, 2015, nypost.com
"It's the new Village people," author Kevin Fasick
"This guy was a Wall St. big," by Shawn Cohen, Kathleen Culliton, and Bruce Golding.
Priscilla DeGregory "The Bums Out"
http://www.azquotes.com/quote/81114
Sojourner Truth http://www.azquotes.com/author/14828-Sojourner Truth
http://www.azquotes.com/author/14828-Sojourner Truth
Sojourner Truth http://www.azquotes.com/author/14828-Sojourner Truth
"Homelessness declining" (Star –Ledger Sunday, June 21, 2015).

Quick Facts April1, 2010
Newark city, New Jersey
North Jersey.com "Homeless epidemic"
White alone, percent, April 1, 2010 (a) 26.3%
New Jersey/ Newark

Black or African American alone, percent, April 1, 2010 (a) 52.4%
books@bookdaily.com
NOTE TO THE READERS

THE AUTHOR INVITES YOU TO DONATE MONEY TO THE NEEDY, PURCHASE A COPY OF THIS BOOK OR SHARE YOUR RESPONSE to the message of this book by contacting her at,

williamsonmarie240@yahoo.com
williamsonmarie240@gmail.com
or call 862-276-7427 to order a copy.
Goodread.com
Facebook
Instagram
Twitter

Google
Marie Williamson Life And Transformational Business Coach

Google
Marie Williamson Eagle Wings Business Coach

Radio Host- Live In The Moment! You Have Not Seen Anything Yet!
WMTR AM RADIO 1250

For Zoom speaking engagements:
Please call (862) 276-7427

-GOD'S ANGELS IN DISGUISE-
"BLESSED IS HE WHO CONSIDERS THE POOR FOR IN THE
TIME OF TROUBLE HE SALLL BE DELIVERED."
He will give His angels charge over us to keep us in all our ways (91).